What People are Saying About *Asking*

Andrea Kihlstedt's Asking Styles construct is _____ fundraising world. It helps each of us to rec_____ strengths in promoting the causes we care about. Share this _____ members, CEOs, staff members... anyone who can help further your cause.

Paula J. Peter
President of The Solstice Group and Co-founder of the Ithaca Institute

It was like a smack on the side of the head! When I read Asking Styles *it occurred to me for the first time—everyone who asks for a gift has a style of their own. And when you determine your style, you will be more confident in asking. More effective. And more successful. Bingo!*

Jerry Panas
Author, Executive Partner, Jerold Panas, Linzy & Partners

New ideas don't come around very often. And this is a revolutionary new idea. Now fundraisers can be shy, introverted, creative, a Mission Controller, a Go-Getter...and every one of them can find the way to ask that suits them best.

Gail Perry
Fired Up Fundraising

Knowing that I am a Kindred Spirit has made a tremendous difference in my day-to-day fundraising work and outlook on asking for gifts. It's allowed me to use the talents I already possess and given me the confidence I need to ask more comfortably and successfully.

Amanda Swan
Gifts Officer, State University of New York at New Paltz

Andrea Kihlstedt wrote the book on capital campaigns. Then she wrote the book on how even novices can raise $1 million. And now she's written the book on pain-free asking. This is for anyone who feels faint at the thought of asking for a gift.

Tom Ahern
Ahern Communications

I was so engrossed with Asking Styles: Harness Your Personal Fundraising Power *that I read it in one sitting. The whole time I was taking notes, even though I've been asking for money, and training others, for the last couple decades!*

Marc A. Pitman
Author of *Ask Without Fear*; Founder, FundraisingCoach.com

What People are Saying about *Asking Styles...* (Cont'd)

I've always been a bit of an introvert and, as a fundraiser, I used to worry that I somehow didn't match up to more outgoing people who appear so much at ease in a group. When I read this eye-opening book on Asking Styles, the truth about my own style hit me like a ton of bricks. Shy fundraisers unite! Your abilities to listen and empathize with others are some of the most effective skills anyone can have.

Pamela Grow
PamelaGrow.com

It's usually the asking part that scares board members and staff, too. Fundraisers do solicitor training, hoping that will make the difference. But, too often, it doesn't. Now Andrea explains our inner selves and how that self can do the all-important asking. This handy little book translates asking into the ways each of us is already most comfortable. Easy to read. Easy to explore with your colleagues. Now you really can just do it.

Simone P. Joyaux, ACFRE
Joyaux Associates, www.simonejoyaux.com

Andrea Kihlstedt is a teacher with great warmth and boundless energy. She approaches each person she meets with respect and curiosity. Those qualities are evident in the pages of this book. If your ambition goes beyond wanting to be comfortable—if you want your fundraising to be authentic— Andrea and this book are wonderful guides.

Paul Jolly
Jump Start Growth, Inc.

If you've ever worked closely with people—or thought you might someday— you can richly benefit from Andrea Kihlstedt's impactful new book. Her people insights are spot on, her fundraising acumen is evident, and her ability to communicate is enviable. My only complaint: I wish I could have drawn from this well of knowledge three decades ago!

Kent Stroman
Author, *Asking about Asking*; Speaker; Fundraising Consultant

My passion has always been to make everyone comfortable with the "thought of raising money" and then find their individual rhythm, so that they will be open to new approaches to asking for money. My fellow author Andrea has written this book to make, as she says, "the ask authentic." It is a terrific resource to have for people who may need a more in-depth analysis of what is, or what can be, their own asking voice, their own Asking Style.

Laura Fredricks
Author of *The ASK*

Asking Styles

Harness Your Personal Fundraising Power

Andrea Kihlstedt

Asking Styles: Harness Your Personal Fundraising Power

One of the In the Trenches™ series

Published by

CharityChannel Press, an imprint of CharityChannel LLC
30021 Tomas, Suite 300
Rancho Santa Margarita, CA 92688-2128 USA
charitychannel.com

In the Trenches™, In the Trenches logo, and book design are trademarks of CharityChannel Press, an imprint of CharityChannel LLC.

Asking Matters and Asking Styles are trademarks of Andrian LLC and are registered or pending in the United States.

ISBN: 978-1-938077-05-0

Library of Congress Control Number: 2012954256

13 12 11 10 9 8 7 6 5 4 3 2

Printed in the United States of America

This and most CharityChannel Press books are available at special quantity discounts for bulk purchases for sales promotions, premiums, fundraising, or educational use. For information, contact CharityChannel Press, 30021 Tomas, Suite 300, Rancho Santa Margarita, CA 92688-2128 USA. +1 949-589-5938.

About the Author

Andrea Kihlstedt has been a fundraising professional for more than three decades. She has degrees in Philosophy from both the University of Pennsylvania and Brown University.

Andrea has a long-standing fascination with human behavior. She is a graduate of the Johns Hopkins Fellows Program in Change Management and she has taken courses at the Gestalt International Study Center where she has also served as a faculty member.

In fundraising, Andrea was a capital campaign consultant for many years, working with organizations large and small. Using her experience in the field, she wrote *Capital Campaigns: Strategies that Work*, which has become a standard text for many fundraising courses. She then wrote *How to Raise $1 Million (or More!) in 10 Bite-Sized Steps* which synthesizes the key lessons of capital campaign fundraising for board members and other volunteers.

Most recently, she co-founded Asking Matters, an innovative website at www.AskingMatters.com dedicated to helping people find the courage they need to get out and ask for gifts in person.

Andrea lives in New York City with her husband, Tyko. She now spends much of her time speaking to and training groups around the country, sharing her ideas and thoughts about fundraising and human motivation.

Dedication

I dedicate this book to three people without whom it would not be.

First, to Asking Matters cofounder, Brian Saber. From the beginning of our discussions about creating a new website, Brian realized how important the concept of Asking Styles could be. Through our joint project, www.AskingMatters.com, he has helped develop and bring this material to life.

Second, to Jezra Kaye, who opened my eyes to the thinking and theory of personality styles and has generously shared her expertise and insights into how personality theory might apply to fundraising.

And finally, I dedicate this book to my husband, Tyko, who was the model for the Mission Controller Asking Style. From him, I have learned the importance of appreciating other people's strengths—particularly when they are not one's own.

Author's Acknowledgments

I am grateful to my colleague Brian Saber, with whom I created Asking Matters. As I was developing my thinking about personal asking styles, Brian encouraged me wholeheartedly, and suggested that this material become the centerpiece of AskingMatters.com. Brian has helped me hone and refine the material on the website and serves as a wonderful spokesman for Kindred Spirits everywhere.

This book would not exist without my writing partner Jezra Kaye, who not only helped me shape my ideas into a clear and well-organized manuscript, but also plied me with strong coffee and delicious desserts while doing so.

I would never have even thought about Asking Styles if I hadn't worked with so many wonderful people over the years who helped me understand. In particular, I wish to thank Megan Hodges, Mary Hedahl, Rich Berlin, Brigid Ganley, Xan Blake, Carol Wishcamper, Carole Gravagno, Paula Peter, Charlie Trautmann, Pamela Grow, Alison Kear, Peter Heller, and Paul Jolly.

Thanks also to Bob Jud who, years ago, introduced me to the idea of axes and quadrants as a way to understand human behavior. And a big hug to Stephen Nill and the excellent editorial team at CharityChannel Press for taking my manuscript seriously and doing a wonderful job of making sure the details were right.

Finally, I acknowledge my family—my husband Tyko, the model Mission Controller who continues to love me even when I am my most Go-Getterish self, and my daughters Rya and Carla, who are always my inspiration.

Publisher's Acknowledgments

This book was produced by a team dedicated to excellence; please send us your feedback to editors@charitychannel.com.

We first wish to acknowledge the tens of thousands of peers who call charitychannel.com their online professional home. Your enthusiastic support for the **In the Trenches**™ series is the wind in our sails.

Members of the team who produced this book include:

Editors

Acquisitions Editor: Linda Lysakowski

Comprehensive Editor: Amy Eisenstein

Copy Editor: Susan Schaefer

Production

In the Trenches Series Design: Deborah Perdue

Layout Editor: Jill McLain

Graphics: Kurt Bigenho, Willa Tracosas

Proofreaders: Linda Lysakowski, Amy Eisenstein, Susan Schaefer, Jill McLain, Stephen Nill

Administrative

CharityChannel LLC: Stephen C. Nill, CEO

Marketing and Public Relations: John Millen

Promotional Videos: Harry McAlister

Contents

Chapter Nine

Foreword

As an author, speaker, and consultant on the topic of fundraising, I am constantly looking for new and exciting ways of making fundraising easier and more enjoyable for board and staff members. In *Asking Styles*, Andrea has hit the nail on the head.

She's created a simple system that helps people ask for gifts in the way that suits them best.

In this remarkable little volume, Andrea debunks the myth that there's one right way to ask for gifts. Instead, she shows you how you can harness your natural strengths to ask in a way that suits you best. And she explains how you can create the kind of authentic conversations that are the "real stuff" of great fundraising.

This book is for board members who feel uncomfortable talking about money; for development directors who are squeamish around people who might be older, wiser, and wealthier than they are; and for executive directors who just don't know where to start.

While facilitating board retreats, I've heard an endless number of excuses from both staff and board members about why they don't ask people for money. In this short, easy-to-follow guide, you will learn that being yourself is the key to success. You'll also learn how to partner with people who don't share your style and how to identify and accommodate a donor's style.

As a consultant and fundraiser, I have learned so much from Andrea over the years. Her experience with capital campaigns and expertise on fundraising are extraordinary. And now I've learned that I'm a Rainmaker—goal-oriented, attentive to details, and excited by my interactions with others. I guess I always knew that, but now Andrea has clarified how it relates to fundraising in a way I'd never thought of before now.

I am delighted that she has written this book to help board and staff members ask with confidence! In a field in which the basics seldom change, Andrea has provided something new, fresh, and extremely useful.

Amy Eisenstein, CFRE
Author, *50 Asks in 50 Weeks* and *Raising More with Less*

Introduction

The Birth of an Idea

Most big ideas come from frustration, and the idea that people have different Asking Styles is no exception. I spent twenty-five years training people to ask—working with thousands of people who would later go out to solicit gifts, running dozens of fundraising trainings, and writing two books on fundraising—before I finally admitted to myself that something just wasn't working well.

I'd been noticing for years that, after a typical fundraising training, half of the participants would leave feeling energized and excited. That was the good news.

The bad news was the other half would leave feeling drained, discouraged, and even more certain that they didn't have what it takes to be a successful solicitor (someone who asks for donations).

I began to wonder why so many people think, *I just can't ask for gifts.* Is that real? Is that true? Or, am I just missing something?

The book that you're about to read is my answer to those questions.

It came out of my belief that the fundraising field doesn't do a good job of helping people use the many natural strengths that they bring to the table.

There are as many ways to solicit gifts as there are people, and if we want fundraisers to be authentic—if authenticity is the heart of the solicitation process—we need to help people learn to ask *in the way that suits them best.*

Why Authenticity Is So Important

Authenticity is the core of successful fundraising.

That's because putting on a front and trying to be someone you are not is contrary to what this business is about.

What *Is* This Fundraising Business About?

Fundraising is about helping your donors achieve *their* goals.

Although some people might still believe that fundraising is about getting other people to do what *you* want them to do, the exact opposite is true: it's about getting to know people well enough and thoroughly enough that you understand what *they* want to do—and can help them to do it.

principle

People who make really generous gifts—who make real investments in an organization—do so because they strongly believe in your organization's mission. Often these beliefs go back to people's childhood experiences or personal, family, or religious values.

If you push a generous donor hard enough, you'll find that there's a story explaining their connection, either to that particular organization or to the mission.

Talk to people who are interested in *homelessness*. There's something, large or small, in their background that leads them to that particular issue.

People who are interested in *art* have something in their experience that connects them to art, and makes them believe it's important enough to invest in.

Your task, as a fundraiser, is not to convince someone who's not interested that they should be. It's to discover people's interests, and—if their interests are truly a good match—to work with them so that they can make the world a better place *through your organization.*

Swing for the Fences

Often, with lower-level gifts, we spend a lot of time and energy just *getting money* from people.

But that sort of transactional approach is seldom the most satisfying kind of fundraising for you, your organization, or your donors.

Fundraising is much more fun (and rewarding) and creates a lasting impact when you can connect on issues a donor truly values, and give that donor the double satisfaction of enjoying a personal interest or passion *while also doing good.*

Helping a donor in this way is a privilege. And if you want to do it successfully, you can't be false, or put on airs. You can't try to be someone else; you can only be yourself!

A Note to Readers

This book was written by a Go-Getter (that's one of the four Asking Styles). As you read on, you'll find that Go-Getters like big, sweeping ideas—and that's what this system is. Asking Styles are simple, clear, and easy to remember. At a glance, you'll be able to grasp the core principles, and apply them to your work, every day.

A Home Run for Harlem RBI

Harlem RBI is a successful nonprofit in East Harlem, New York, that's organized around baseball.

Its goal is not to create baseball players, but to use the game to help young people learn about values, teamwork, and overcoming tough odds (because the odds, when you step up to the plate, are stacked pretty high against you).

Kids sign up for the ball teams that Harlem RBI fields, but they stay for the learning and mentoring that accompany the after-school games. And board members sign on to help young people, and also, importantly, because of what baseball has meant in their own lives.

That's why New York Yankees' first baseman Mark Teixeira has been such a powerful addition to Harlem RBI's board. He comes from a family of teachers, and his passion for education matches his passion for our national pastime. Because he *authentically* embodies everything that Harlem RBI strives to achieve, his presence on the board has energized the entire organization in a way that other celebrities—perhaps even other ballplayers—would not have been able to achieve.

 stories from the real world

Asking Styles don't explain everything about everyone. They aren't "all you need to get by" to be a successful staff member, board member, or nonprofit executive. They won't solve your every challenge. But understanding Asking Styles will provide insight into how the people around you function, and will help you perform more effectively yourself.

principle

If you like intuitive systems, you will probably revel in this one. If your approach is more analytical, you might want to explore these ideas further, adding detail from your own experience and validation from the large body of research that has been done on personality styles.

Whatever the case, please keep in mind that this Asking Styles system intentionally simplifies the complex study of human nature. Its purpose is not to expand the field of psychology, but to give you a tool you can use right now.

Chapter One

One Size Doesn't Fit All

IN THIS CHAPTER

- ┈➤ Is there an ideal fundraiser?
- ┈➤ Understanding introverted versus extroverted, and analytic versus intuitive, personalities
- ┈➤ The value of each Asking Style

When I started thinking about Asking Styles, I wanted to create a system that was simple and easy to remember. My hope was that people would (a) identify their own style (and remember its name!), and (b) understand all four styles clearly enough that they could recognize the styles in others.

I didn't set out to create a big psychological system. Instead, I wanted to create something that people could hang onto. Something that would inspire them to say, "I can do this work, and I can do it in a way that's going to suit me. I don't have to be a super salesperson. I can be *me*."

But in order to do that, I needed to get better at understanding how to use people's strengths for fundraising.

Specifically, I started wondering:

- ◆ Why, when the best experts on soliciting gifts train staff members and volunteers, do we inspire only *some* of them to actually get out and ask?

The "Ideal" Fundraiser?

Lots of people in the fundraising business think that one particular type of person makes an ideal fundraiser. They might think of the ideal fundraiser as a man who is outgoing and friendly. He's handsome with white teeth, a broad smile, and black hair. He's wearing a beautifully detailed Armani sport jacket.

He's also an articulate, convincing, and courageous spokesperson for the organization. He knows exactly the right words for any situation, and has every fact and figure at his fingertips. He's comfortable talking about money, and is not afraid to ask.

Or it might be a tall, slim, blonde woman…

Unfortunately, or maybe fortunately, neither of these people is real. So, rather than emulate the ideal, doesn't it make more sense for you to embrace your own Asking Style, and ask in a way that will work for *you*?

principle

- ◆ Why are so many people afraid or even convinced that they don't have "the right skill set" for soliciting donors?

- ◆ Are we putting out the message that there's "one right way" to ask for gifts? One ideal type of fundraiser?

The Missing Puzzle Piece

One night, as I was pondering these questions, I happened to glance across the living room at my husband Tyko.

Tyko is a retired professor of art and architectural history, and his personality is what you might expect from a lifelong academic. He's quiet, prone to evaluating things (and other people!), and not much given to excess drama or hyperbole.

And I found myself wondering if this quiet, self-contained, matter-of-fact man could ever successfully solicit a gift.

On the surface, it didn't seem likely, since his personality runs counter to how successful fundraisers are *supposed* to act. And yet, I couldn't stop wondering what kind of a fundraiser Tyko would be.

As I thought about it, I realized that he would be the kind of fundraiser who is:

◆ Thorough

◆ Well prepared

◆ Owns the information he's presenting

◆ Doesn't go into the field until he's ready

◆ Thoroughly believes in what he's doing

◆ Makes a solid, logical case

In other words, Tyko would be a natural solicitor for donors who move slowly toward a decision, want to take a logical approach, and back up their giving decisions with *facts*.

Of course, not every donor makes fact-based decisions, and Tyko's presentations might well bore a more emotion-based donor.

But that didn't seem insurmountable. After all, Tyko (or any fundraiser of his type) could be trained to stop talking if a donor's eyes started glazing over. And, he could be paired with a partner whose strength was connecting emotionally.

Many people confuse extroversion with sociability. If you are outgoing, or even highly sociable, you might still be an introvert if you need time alone to recharge after socializing.

important

Sauce for the Goose

When I was done thinking about my husband, I decided to look at myself the same way.

Where Tyko is introverted (someone who's energized by his own private experience), I'm an extrovert who loves being out and about, loves engaging with other people.

Where Tyko is fact-based and analytical, I'm intuitive and so uninterested in facts that, sadly, my eyes *do* glaze over when presented with lots of detail.

So what kind of a fundraiser did that make *me*?

After reflecting, I decided that it makes me the kind of solicitor who can:

- ◆ Energize people and bring them along

- ◆ See the big picture and future possibilities

- ◆ Make a compelling and dramatic case

- ◆ Use words and metaphors to excite and inspire

- ◆ Make whatever is going on fun for myself and others

In other words, I'm the perfect solicitor for donors who want to be moved, want to be excited, and want to connect on a personal level.

But am I the best solicitor for *everyone*?

Clearly, not for people who want facts! *That doesn't mean I can't solicit them—* just that I need to be aware of, and compensate for, our differences. I can do that by bringing a detailed case for support, teaming up with a fact-oriented colleague, or offering to send the facts later.

As long as I'm leading with my strengths, these are compromises that most donors will accept.

Getting a Clue

As I thought this through, I was excited to realize that, professional myths to the contrary, no one is a perfect fundraiser. Conversely, while people solicit in very different ways, you are best able to connect with donors when you do it *your* way, instead of trying to be someone you're not.

The other exciting realization was that, in trying to understand Tyko's style in relation to my own, I had developed a simple way of articulating our differences that might generalize beyond the two of us.

Tyko was most certainly an introvert and analytical by nature. I, on the other hand, am an extrovert and intuitive.

Tyko	Andrea
Introvert	Extrovert
Analytical	Intuitive

I wondered: *Just how useful were those descriptions? Did they apply to everyone? Were there other ways to combine the two qualities? And what kind of fundraisers would people with other combinations of these qualities be?*

It was time to lay out a grid and see!

How You Interact With Others

Extroverts
(talk to think)

EXTROVERT

INTROVERT

Introverts
(think to talk)

Interaction and Information

From my own thinking, and from what I knew of personality systems like DiSC, the Temperament Sorter in David Keirsey's *Please Understand Me II*, and the Myers-Briggs Type Indicator, the first axis on my grid *was how people interact with others.*

Although most people have heard the words "introvert" and "extrovert," there's a lot of confusion about what they mean.

- ◆ *Introverts* can be shy or outgoing, socially awkward or socially sophisticated, but in either case they are energized by their *inner lives,* and don't like to say things they haven't thought through first.

- ◆ *Extroverts* can be shy or outgoing, socially awkward or socially sophisticated, but in either case they are energized by their *social lives,* and often don't know what they're thinking until they hear themselves saying it out loud.

The second axis, again drawn from both experience and theory, is based on how you gather information:

How You Gather Information

Analytic	ANALYTIC	INTUITIVE	Intuitive
(inductive, fact-oriented)			(deductive, idea-oriented)

Here, again, the two styles of taking in information are very different from each other.

Analytics are focused on the past and the present (what has been and is currently true), on "hard" data (facts and figures), and on logical thought processes. They gather information in small bits—lots of them—and build those pieces up to bigger concepts.

Intuitives are focused on the present and the future, on the big picture instead of specific details, and on abstract ideas and concepts. They gather information in broad sweeps, and differentiate into smaller bits later.

It's easy to see how these two styles might clash!

But perhaps you're wondering what information gathering has to do with fundraising in the first place.

❑ Observe how you feel after spending time with a large group of people. Whether or not you enjoyed the experience, are you energized (extrovert) or exhausted (introvert) afterward?

❑ Think about your partner or close friends. Do they seem to be introverted or extroverted? How do you know?

❑ List three of your favorite donors. Do you think they are introverts or extroverts? What clues have they given you?

The short answer is: everything, as you'll see in Chapter Two!

To Recap

◆ There is no such thing as an ideal fundraiser.

◆ The Asking Styles system lets you easily understand and remember your fundraising type.

◆ Asking Styles are based on how you interact with others (introvert or extrovert) and how you gather information (analytically or intuitively).

◆ Every Asking Style can succeed with the right donors.

◆ Understanding *your* style and building on its strengths is the key to success.

Chapter Two

The Four Asking Styles

IN THIS CHAPTER

···➔ Understanding the four Asking Styles

···➔ Identifying your own Asking Style

···➔ The value of being guided by your Asking Style

A s we discussed in Chapter One, people prefer to *interact* with each other in one of two ways:

Introverts like to think before they speak. They're private people who are energized by their *inner lives*.

Extroverts are energized by their *social lives*, and often need to talk to understand what they're thinking.

We also looked at the two ways that people gather *information*:

Analytics prefer to focus on specific data from the past and the present.

Intuitives prefer to focus on future possibilities and big ideas.

Defining the Asking Styles

Once I had figured out the two axes, I put them together to see if the whole was greater than the sum of its parts.

(Hint: It was!)

The combined axes looked like this...

...and yielded these four combinations of qualities:

Analytic + Extrovert	Intuitive + Extrovert
Analytic + Introvert	Intuitive + Introvert

The more I talked to people, tested these categories, and matched them to my own observations, the more strongly I began to feel that they would form a valid basis for a system of Asking Styles.

What's in a Name?

While the categories above resonated for everyone I spoke to, the category *names* did not. (No one wants to hear, or will remember, that the Asking Style category this person fits into is "Analytic + Introvert.")

So I gave each Asking Style a name that reflects its notable characteristics:

◆ Analytic extroverts are *Rainmakers (RM)*—outgoing, objective people who work hard, plan well, and like to be in charge.

◆ Intuitive extroverts are *Go-Getters (GG)*—gregarious, big-picture thinkers who exude charm and energy.

◆ Intuitive introverts are *Kindred Spirits (KS)*—people who lead with their hearts and are inspired by stories of individual success.

◆ Analytic introverts are *Mission Controllers (MC)*—detail-oriented planners who guard against things that might go wrong.

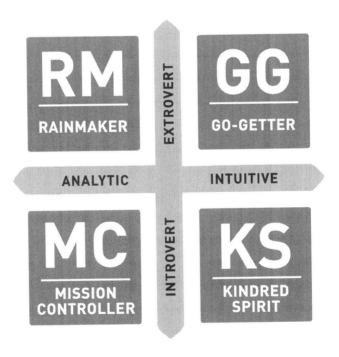

What About Your Donor's Asking Style?

This book contains one chapter about using Asking Styles to connect with donors. But its main focus, as you've already seen, is on how Asking Styles can help you understand *yourself.*

Some people find that very confusing.

They think, "Shouldn't I be focused on *my donor's* personality instead of my own? After all, *I'm* not the person being appealed to!"

The answer to that is yes and no.

Of course you want to understand your donor's needs, wants, interests, background, goals, hot spots, and much, much more. But understanding your donor's *personal style* is less useful than you might think. That's because:

> The Asking Style names were chosen to be accurate, memorable, and distinctive. They aren't comprehensive descriptions of you, nor are they intended to "put you in a box." Instead, they are designed to help you think about asking in a more nuanced way, so that you and your colleagues can ask more effectively.
>
> **principle**

◆ Invariably, when we ask somebody for a gift, we become anxious. And when we are anxious, we revert to the patterns and the ways that are most natural to us. We are far less able to *adapt* who we are—so a strategy based on adapting to others is not going to hold up well under pressure.

◆ Focusing solely on our *donor's* style doesn't solve the main problem that Asking Styles are designed to address: how to support people who are afraid to ask for gifts because they don't think they have the "right" style. If you're not confident about your own style to begin with, trying to change it to fit your donor is not going to improve the situation.

◆ And finally, self-knowledge really is the best route to understanding someone else. If you know about Asking Styles, if you understand your own style, and if you observe your donor while the two of you interact, you'll probably get a better understanding of what works and what doesn't work for the donor than you would if you were trying to analyze or mimic the donor's style.

As Polonius said in Shakespeare's *Hamlet*, "This above all; to thine own self be true, and it must follow, as the night the day, thou canst not then be false to any man."

See if you can find your "true self" in the four Asking Styles descriptions that follow:

Kindred Spirits

Kindred Spirits (KS) are *intuitive introverts*. This means that (a) like Go-Getters, they rely less on facts and data and more (much more!) on instinct and ideas; and (b) they are private and internally focused.

Even outgoing Kindred Spirits hold their thoughts and feelings close; but their intuitive nature makes them sensitive to others, and driven to improve other people's lives. They generally prefer to socialize with smaller groups, in quiet settings.

As solicitors, they're strongest when they follow their instincts. Although they're happy to let others speak, they can be quite articulate about things that matter to them. Like Go-Getters, they bring passion to the cause, and connect with donors through their deep commitment.

The question that's often foremost in a Kindred Spirit's mind is: *What moves my heart?* Kindred Spirit are able to overcome shyness with the power of their emotional commitment to the organization. And that heartfelt quality communicates powerfully to donors.

Rainmakers

Rainmakers (RM), as noted above, are *analytic extroverts*. This means that (a) their energy is focused outward, into the world and being with other people; and (b) they like information (data) that is concrete, specific, and real (no hunches, please!).

Rainmakers tend to be goal-oriented and competitive. They often like team sports and find inspiration in the energy of others.

As solicitors, Rainmakers are comfortable talking to anyone. They need as much information as possible about the donor and the cause so they can lay out a clear and objective case. Of the four *Asking Styles*, they have the greatest ability to adapt to other people's styles, and will use this skill to connect with donors.

The question that's often foremost in a Rainmaker's mind is: *What is the goal?* A Rainmaker will want to know how much the organization is trying to raise and how the specific request fits into that goal.

Mission Controllers

Mission Controllers (MC) are *analytic introverts.* This means that (a) like Rainmakers, they prefer their data to be measurable and specific; and (b) their energy is pointed inward, making them more reflective, cautious, and slower to speak.

Mission Controllers are often relied on by others, because of their insistence that things be done thoroughly and well. They have great respect for history, and generally look ahead primarily to envision and avoid potential problems.

As solicitors, they make objective strategy decisions, and connect with donors by laying out a thorough and detailed presentation. Private and quietly thoughtful, they require a wealth of information and need time to process and analyze.

The question that's often foremost in a Mission Controller's mind is: *What might go wrong?* Mission Controllers believe in doing things right and want to head off problems before they occur.

Go-Getters

Go-Getters (GG) are *intuitive extroverts.* This means that (a) they will accept information from any source, including their own imaginations, and are more comfortable with big ideas than with detailed data; and (b) they love to interact with others.

Go-Getters are forward-looking and willing to take leaps of faith. They are more inclined to big gestures than subtlety, and can use their creative energy to shape compelling visions of what might be.

Stifled by the Script

Brigid G., the development director of a charter school group, was getting ready to call on a past donor. In preparation, she sat with one of her staff members and created a script for the phone call. Then she picked up the phone. When Jack answered, Brigid launched right into her "pitch," reading from the notes in front of her. When she finally finished talking, Jack said that he was too busy to meet, and gave no avenue for future contact. Brigid hung up the phone and let that hollow feeling of having blown it sweep through her.

Then Brigid realized what she'd done wrong: she'd forgotten to be herself. Though she didn't know this at the time, Brigid is a Go-Getter (an intuitive extrovert), and is strongest when she stays in the moment, not when she's following a pre-planned script. By trying to act like someone else, Brigid had lost her own asking edge. An awareness of her own Asking Style would have saved her from making this mistake.

As solicitors, Go-Getters are strongest when they follow their instincts—like Brigid, in the following Story from the Real World. They thrive on being with other people, are passionate about everything they do, and connect with donors through charisma and high energy.

The question that's often foremost in a Go-Getter's mind is: *What is the opportunity?* A Go-Getter is less focused on the dollar goal and more interested in doors that might open as a result of a conversation with a donor.

If You're Still Not Sure About Your Asking Style

Not everyone thinks about Asking Styles in the "compare and contrast" way above.

If you're a more detail-oriented person, take the little assessment on the next page and see if a clearer picture of your style emerges.

What's Your Asking Style?

Instructions for the assessment

1. Read each question.

2. If it's true for you, circle both T's in the row.

3. If it's false for you, circle both F's in the row.

4. Add the number of circles in each column and indicate totals in the bottom row.

Questions	R	G	K	M
I have a good memory for facts and figures.	T	F	F	T
I use the energy of others to spark my thinking.	T	T	F	F
I usually form my ideas before I speak.	F	F	T	T
Once I make a decision, I usually stick with it.	T	F	F	T
I am at my best when I am spontaneous.	F	T	T	F
I hesitate before introducing myself to others.	F	F	T	T
I have the patience for step-by-step work.	T	F	F	T
I act from my heart as much as I do from my head.	F	T	T	F
Goals are important to me.	T	F	F	T
I adapt readily to the style of others.	F	T	T	F
I make sure I have time alone to recharge.	F	F	T	T
I tend to make up my mind quickly.	T	T	F	F
Number of Circles in Each Column	R=	G=	K=	M=

Adapted from a full online assessment at www.AskingMatters.com.

Calculate Your Asking Style

Your R Score _____ Rainmaker
Your G Score _____ Go-Getter
Your K Score _____ Kindred Spirit
Your M Score _____ Mission Controller

Primary Style (highest score) _____

Secondary Style (next highest) _____

If you have equal scores in two styles, you should read both chapters and decide which fits you best.

If you identify strongly with more than one Asking Style, remember that all of us function differently in response to the demands of different situations.

You may be a Go-Getter who is required to act like a Mission Controller on your job. Or perhaps you're a Kindred Spirit who's learned to be so assertive that you're now mistaken for a Rainmaker.

Even if you function well in two or more styles, it's likely that, underneath it all, you have a *primary* Asking Style that, like your *core self*, remains the same.

important

Let Your Asking Style Be Your Guide

Now that you have a sense of your Asking Style, it's time to look at the way that style can help you solicit more effectively.

I believe that there are five key stages of asking for a gift and that your Asking Style plays a role in how you can best approach *each* one.

The five steps are:

1. Selecting who to ask

2. Getting ready to ask

3. Setting up the meeting

4. Asking for a gift

5. Following through

In the chapters that follow, you'll find ways to think about, prepare for, and execute each of those steps:

◆ If you are a *Kindred Spirit*, turn to Chapter Three.

◆ If you are a *Rainmaker*, turn to Chapter Four.

◆ If you are a *Mission Controller*, turn to Chapter Five.

◆ If you are a *Go-Getter*, turn to Chapter Six.

❑ Read the chapter that describes your *Asking Style*.

❑ Then read the other three chapters.

❑ For each of the styles that is not your own, identify a colleague, board member, or direct report who fits the description.

❑ Make a list of ways you can work with this person that would benefit from the difference in your styles.

To Recap

◆ The four Asking Styles are: *Rainmakers* (analytic extroverts), *Go-Getters* (intuitive extroverts), *Kindred Spirits* (intuitive introverts), and *Mission Controllers* (analytic introverts).

◆ "To thine own self be true." You are more likely to succeed by relying on your own style's strengths than trying to match your donor's presumed style.

◆ Your style plays a role in how you approach each of the five stages of an ask: selecting who to ask, preparing to ask, setting up the meeting, asking for a gift, and following through.

Chapter Three

How Kindred Spirits Ask

IN THIS CHAPTER

- ···→ Understanding Kindred Spirits

- ···→ How Kindred Spirits select who to ask, get ready to ask, set up the meeting, ask for a gift, and follow through

- ···→ Practical tips for Kindred Spirits

P aul J. is now a fundraising consultant, but he has been a development professional and a volunteer for several religious and social justice organizations. Paul takes his beliefs seriously. They are core to the way he does business. In fact, they are core to the way he lives. A Quaker, Paul is a pacifist with a strong sense of fairness and equality.

And yes, Paul is on the quiet side. You'd be unlikely to see Paul "working the room." Instead, you'll find him deep in thoughtful conversation with one or two people in the corner.

Paul does not match our stereotype of "the perfect fundraiser." He isn't gregarious, doesn't wade into the thick of things, and values harmony in his relationships above "winning."

Yet Paul is a first-rate fundraiser. Like many other Kindred Spirits (and they are common in the profession, which is, after all, about helping others), he can deploy a quiet power that is often unassailable. That power comes from Paul's ability to connect with a donor's heart, and from his passionate commitment to the causes he believes in.

That commitment comes through loud and clear when Paul asks for a gift—and so does his warmth and interest in the person he's talking to. Like many introverts, Paul isn't motivated to seek center stage but is comfortable sitting back and listening to his donors. And while *listening* isn't the "flashiest" skill, it turns out to be a critical success factor for anyone who solicits gifts.

If you, like Paul, are a Kindred Spirit (introverted and intuitive), you will probably:

- ◆ Be understated, sensitive, and attentive to others

- ◆ Be private and quietly thoughtful

- ◆ Make decisions based on instinct

- ◆ Bring your passion to your cause

- ◆ Connect with others through your own commitment

Let's look at how Kindred Spirits function as solicitors.

How a Kindred Spirit Selects Who to Ask

If you're a Kindred Spirit, you've got lots of heart—and your heart gives you the courage to ask for things that you believe are important. Still, you might find it hard to hear people say "no." When someone disagrees with you, you might feel more inclined to draw back, in the interest of harmony, than to jump into a heated discussion.

This love of harmony suggests that you are strongest when soliciting prospects who share your beliefs and commitment—people, in other words, who are already inclined to give. While Rainmakers and Go-Getters enjoy the challenge of winning over skeptics, you will be more engaged (and thus more successful) in relationships that are based on authentically shared values and passions.

That same desire for authenticity can, however, make it hard for Kindred Spirits to solicit their closest friends or relatives, lest they be perceived as "using" or "pressuring" the people they love. If this is your case, once again, follow your heart: ignore the suggestion that you "just get over it" and let others solicit your friends and family.

Finally, think small when you're picking who to ask. Select a couple of prospects for now (you can always come back for more names later). While a giant spreadsheet with a dozen names will energize extroverted fundraisers, you're energized by interacting with a very few individuals at one time.

How a Kindred Spirit Gets Ready to Ask

As a Kindred Spirit, you are probably not drawn to facts, figures, and details. So put together a page of salient facts—things that your donor is likely to ask about—and be sure to have that reference sheet with you when you meet with a donor. You might include key budget figures, numbers of people served, the current amount in your endowment fund, the fundraising goal, and other important facts. No need to memorize them; just pull out the fact sheet if it turns out that you're talking to someone who asks for that information.

Selecting Who to Ask

◆ Select prospects who are already committed to your cause.

◆ Ask others to solicit your friends and relatives if you prefer to not do so yourself.

◆ Focus on a couple of prospects at a time, then go back for more names.

practical tip

Getting Ready to Ask

◆ Have a fact sheet you can pull out if your donor asks for data.

◆ Be ready to offer specific stories and personal experiences that illustrate the impact of your organization's work.

◆ Understand your donor as an individual, and prepare to ask questions that renew the donor's connection to your cause.

practical tip

With the facts thus covered, you can focus on your strong suit: discussing values and mission. Think about why your organization is so important, and summarize your ideas in a few simple bullet points. Pick a few stories that illustrate the impact of your organization's work, and practice delivering them concisely and with confidence. If no stories come to mind, spend a bit of time with the program directors, or even in the field, and notice the moments that move your heart. These personal observations will support and inspire your passion, and are likely to stir a response in your donor.

Spend a bit of time getting to know your prospective donors before you go see them. Familiarize yourself with their bios, and as much as you can learn about their families, hobbies, and personal lives. You'll also want to prepare some questions that refresh your donor's sense of commitment, like:

- ◆ What got you started as a donor to this organization?

- ◆ How did you get connected to this organization?

- ◆ Have you been to see our program recently?

- ◆ How would you like to be more involved?

Because Kindred Spirits sometimes find negotiations stressful, be sure to decide on a specific dollar amount to ask for *before* you contact the donor. Making this decision in advance will free you to enjoy the conversation, and focus on connecting with your donor instead of anticipating the ask itself.

How a Kindred Spirit Sets Up the Meeting

Because they sometimes take "no" personally, many Kindred Spirits hesitate to pick up the phone and ask for a meeting. If this describes you, consider sending a letter (by email, or the old-fashioned way) to tell the donor why you'd like to get together in person and that you'll be in touch next week to schedule a meeting.

Once you've sent a letter, of course, you've got no choice but to follow up with a call or email to schedule the meeting. If you find yourself procrastinating or feeling that you don't want to "impose," ask your friends and colleagues for support. (One Kindred Spirit client of mine asks her colleague, "Check to make sure I've followed up!") And use email to communicate if you prefer; the goal here is to *schedule a meeting*, not to make yourself pick up the phone.

Because you will be contacting people who have a proven interest in the cause, it's likely they will be happy to meet with you. Some, however, might ask if you can handle your meeting over the phone. While it's easy to agree to that, ample evidence shows that meeting in person leads to a richer conversation, and is likely to result in a larger gift. Meeting people in person will give you the opportunity to get to know your donors better.

You'll be able to see how they live, connect with them personally, and get a much clearer sense of how you might engage them in your organization. So be sure that you're prepared to counter that request, perhaps by saying that *you* look forward to meeting in person so you can have a more in-depth talk.

Setting Up the Meeting

◆ If you're not fond of picking up the phone, send your donor an email or letter telling the donor why you want to meet.

◆ Ask your friends and colleagues to help if you tend to procrastinate about follow-up.

◆ Be prepared to insist on meeting with your donor in person. It really does make a difference!

 practical tip

How a Kindred Spirit Asks for a Gift

Before you go out to ask (and this suggestion applies to every Asking Style!), I recommend reviewing the qualities that make you so well qualified to succeed.

As a Kindred Spirit, you are especially skilled at listening to and empathizing with others. Never doubt that these talents are a gift *to your donors*. In other words: Who else invites them to discuss the hopes or life lessons that inspire their gifts? How often do they get to speak about the role that giving plays in their lives? And when was the last time they got to sit and share their thoughts about your organization?

Asking for a Gift

◆ Don't worry about making a "presentation." Instead, share your feelings about the organization, and then let the donor respond.

◆ Remember that, while specifying an amount may feel uncomfortable, it's a key element of the solicitation process.

◆ Consider bringing a partner with you who can help you close the gift.

practical tip

Remember that the best solicitations are not glossy presentations; they are conversations about shared values in which the donor plays at least as big a role as the solicitor. Similarly, the best fundraisers do not talk donors *into* making a gift. By activating their donors' motivations, they allow donors to *talk themselves* into giving gifts that are close to their hearts. They *listen* donors into giving—and Kindred Spirits are great listeners!

Kindred Spirits and the Five-Part Ask

A well-designed ask usually has five parts. After reviewing your fundraising strengths, you might want to think about each of these before you begin your solicitation.

Introduction

This early portion of a meeting gives you a chance to focus the attention of your donor, and find common ground through a discussion of everyday topics. If you feel any nervousness around the visit, getting started might be the most challenging part. Some Kindred Spirits find that mentioning their discomfort with the process is a good way to put themselves at ease. Others focus on their donor, and lose the self-consciousness they might feel by putting *the other person* at ease.

Dialogue

This important part of the ask relies on your ability to pose open-ended questions that draw prospects into a discussion of how they relate to your organization. Prepare some questions in advance to help you get the conversation started. From there, your natural empathy will guide the way.

Presentation

As a Kindred Spirit, all you have to do to make the case is to tell the donor why you care. Plan to talk *for just three minutes* about how the organization has affected your life, or tell a program story. For you, it's not about facts and figures; it's simply and fully about making a difference. Another way to look at this is: you don't really have to present at all! Just briefly share your commitment and passion for the cause, and then give your donor time to respond.

Ask

This is the one sentence you should memorize in advance: "Would you consider making a gift of $_____to this project?"

If, as with most Kindred Spirits, you dislike hearing "no," it would be easy for you to succumb to the temptation of not specifying an amount—so prepare this part of the ask in advance, and steel yourself against that temptation. (You may *alter* the amount you ask for, based on things you learn during the conversation, but don't go in without a number.) And be sure to wait however long it takes for your donor to respond. Don't jump in and make the prospect "comfortable" by equivocating on your ask.

Close

This can be the most difficult step for Kindred Spirits, who are often averse to putting others "on the spot." Unfortunately, if a donor perceives that you're uncomfortable about closing, the donor might use that as an excuse to postpone making a firm commitment. So either discipline yourself to get a clear decision on the gift (or next steps), or bring a colleague to handle this part of the process. Remember, your organization is much too important to leave this critical step to chance!

How a Kindred Spirit Follows Through

Be sure to write a personal note of thanks immediately after your solicitation. If your donor has made a gift, highlight the importance of that gift not just to the organization, but also to you. And if your donor has said "no," pay even *more* attention to your note of thanks. Let your donor know that you fully understand the decision, and look forward to staying in touch.

Of course, every gift also needs a formal response that thanks the donor, reiterates the specifics, and includes a tax receipt. Be sure to communicate with your organization's staff so that this paperwork goes out within a day or two of the gift. (It's easy to neglect this follow-up task if you aren't paying attention.)

You'll also want to follow up personally with your donor. You can do this with an email thank-you, followed by more personal written correspondence.

Remember that, whatever happened at this visit, you are building relationships for the long term. Many of the people you ask are likely to be good friends of the organization and might well become your friends over time. You might connect with them at organizational events throughout the year, or choose to visit them year after year as your relationships mature.

Following Through

◆ Write a personal note to thank your donor for the visit, *whether or not* the prospect made a gift.

❏ Read Chapters Four through Six to better understand Rainmakers, Mission Controllers, and Go-Getters.

❏ Write down three ways that you could work more effectively with colleagues who have each Asking Style.

❏ Make a list of the six people with whom you work most closely. What do you think their Asking Styles are?

❏ Spend some time with each of these people, talking about your style and theirs.

❏ Identify three ways that your styles complement each other and three things that are likely to rub one or both of you the wrong way.

❏ If you're working with specific donors, write down what you believe their styles to be, and list three things that you will do to accommodate each of their styles.

◆ Make sure that your organization's official thanks and your donor's tax receipt go out within a few days of your visit.

◆ Stay in touch with your donors throughout the year, so that your relationships with them (and their connections to your organization) grow.

To Recap

◆ Kindred Spirits are introverted intuitives, who value interpersonal harmony, and don't like to hear "no." They are especially well suited to asking donors who share their deeply-held values, and have already shown a willingness to give.

◆ If, like most Kindred Spirits, you're indifferent to facts and figures, create a "cheat sheet" to refer to when donors want this information. Also prepare some stories and anecdotes that move *your* heart and illustrate the impact of your organization's mission.

◆ Because you approach asking with intuition and insight, don't worry about giving a presentation—and *don't* "talk your donor into the gift." Instead, use your listening skills and empathy to tap your donor's own motivation. Donors will talk themselves into giving.

Chapter Four

How Rainmakers Ask

IN THIS CHAPTER

- ┈➔ Understanding Rainmakers

- ┈➔ How Rainmakers select who to ask, get ready to ask, set up the meeting, ask for a gift, and follow through

- ┈➔ Practical tips for Rainmakers

Dave B. is the executive director of a rapidly growing youth development organization. A large component of Dave's job is fundraising—and he keeps his eye on the money ball.

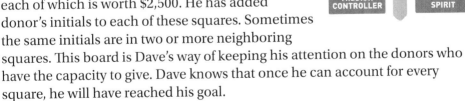

Hanging on the wall in front of Dave's desk is a whiteboard that he's divided into small squares, each of which is worth $2,500. He has added donor's initials to each of these squares. Sometimes the same initials are in two or more neighboring squares. This board is Dave's way of keeping his attention on the donors who have the capacity to give. Dave knows that once he can account for every square, he will have reached his goal.

Dave is a true Rainmaker. He's goal oriented. He's systematic. He's strategic. And he's also very personable. It's seldom that he's not emailing or speaking with one donor or another. For Dave, each gift results from many (often dozens) contacts with the donor.

Many of Dave's colleagues are mystified by his systematic approach to fundraising, since they know him to be a person who's also passionately committed to doing good. How, they wonder, can he be so warm and spontaneous with the children in his programs, yet so focused and driven with its donors?

The answer to this seeming paradox lies in Dave's combination of extroverted energy and analytical decision making. As an extrovert, he relishes getting out into the fray, and is not inclined to second-guess—let alone agonize about—his own motives or relationships with donors. As an analytic thinker, Dave's strength is devising and following a plan; he takes a practical approach, and will literally "check off the boxes" until he succeeds.

While Rainmakers like Dave are often lauded as "ideal" fundraisers, it's important to realize that *they are just doing what comes naturally to them*. Your success will likewise come from developing your personal strengths and skills, whatever your Asking Style.

If you, like Dave, are a Rainmaker (analytic and extroverted), you will probably:

- ◆ Base your decisions on information and analysis
- ◆ Feel comfortable talking to anyone
- ◆ Require detailed information
- ◆ Connect by responding to your donor's style
- ◆ Be goal-oriented, strategic, and competitive

Let's look at how Rainmakers function as solicitors.

How a Rainmaker Selects Who to Ask

As a Rainmaker, you have the courage to go for the gold, and ask *those who you think will give the largest gifts*. These might be your personal contacts or people who are already major donors to your organization.

Some people find it difficult to ask their friends, colleagues, and relatives for gifts, but as a Rainmaker, these are natural prospects for you. If you have a sense of why someone might be interested in the cause and you believe that the potential gift is worth the ask, you'll be willing to ask.

You also have the courage to ask people who might say "no." While you don't enjoy being turned down (in fact, you often persist in the face of "no"), being turned down doesn't take the wind out of your sails. You are able to learn from the process and simply move on.

Similarly, you're able to ask for gifts that will encourage people to stretch. You figure that, if you're going to ask for a gift at all, you want that ask to *really* count.

Selecting Who to Ask

◆ Select very high-yield potential donors.

◆ Put your friends, business colleagues, and relatives on your list of prospective donors.

◆ Be willing to select some prospects who are not yet involved with your organization.

Your courage makes you capable of "cold calling" people who are not yet donors, but have related interests. While these calls might require a creativity that pushes you outside your comfort zone, your persistence will make you successful—and you might engage new donors who will give to your organization for years to come.

How a Rainmaker Gets Ready to Ask

As a Rainmaker, you like to be thoroughly prepared. You will feel comfortable if you have reviewed the annual report, the budget, and any information you have about the specific project for which you are raising money.

Getting Ready to Ask

◆ Assemble all the information you can get about your organization and fundraising campaign, including how donors will be recognized.

◆ Use a gift range chart or donor pyramid to put your donors' giving in context.

◆ Use program numbers to make your case, and fundraising numbers to solicit your donors.

If you're working on a fundraising campaign, you'll want to know things such as: What's the goal? What's the timetable? Who's given already? How do the gifts I've solicited compare with those solicited by others? How will my donors be recognized? Will their names appear on a wall plaque by gift amount? Will they appear in the annual report? You will make excellent use of tools like a gift-range chart or donor pyramid that creates a context for your discussion with donors.

Because Rainmakers are analytic by nature, you will make your case with numbers. You'll want to be armed with facts about how many people your organization serves, and by what percentage its programs have grown. But you'll also want to use fundraising numbers. For you, it's easy to tell a prospect, "Gus, we're just $5,000 from our goal. Would you consider putting in $1,000 of that?"

How a Rainmaker Sets Up the Meeting

As extroverts, Rainmakers enjoy directly engaging with people. You have no problem picking up the phone, so use this as your first approach. If you get voice mail, leave a message saying that you called, and will call again. Leave your phone number for a return call, but don't ask the prospect to call you back. Leaving return calls in the hands of the donors puts you in the awkward position of seeming like a nag if they don't return your call.

> Rainmakers instinctively avoid putting themselves in the position of having to wait by the phone for donors to call them back. They might say, "Give me a call if you can," but will add, "or I'll get back to *you* next Monday at 2 p.m."

important

You can precede and follow up the phone call with personal, friendly emails to be sure you're connecting directly with the person you want to ask.

Because you don't want to waste time—either yours or anyone else's—tell people exactly why you would like to visit them, letting them know that you will talk with them about a gift. That way, if they aren't interested, you can move on, and so can they.

If you don't already do this, try giving someone two possible dates and times for a meeting and ask which is better, rather than ask if the person is willing to meet. This is a tried-and-true technique that you'll be comfortable putting into practice.

While you are strategic and goal-oriented, you are also patient. Plan to have several meetings or contacts with a new prospective donor before you are ready to ask for a gift. If you are going to ask for a large gift, your patience is likely to pay off.

How a Rainmaker Asks for a Gift

As a Rainmaker, you will be most successful at soliciting when you combine both sides of your Asking Style: your ability to command the facts and figures to make a strong analytic case, and your ability to be sensitive and responsive to your donor.

Setting Up the Meeting

◆ Dispense with formal proposals. Send personal emails or pick up the phone.

◆ Let your prospects know why you are calling to qualify the meeting in advance.

◆ Take the time to get to know your prospects and help them figure out why they want make a gift.

 practical tip

Set a dollar goal for each of your solicitations. Decide in advance how much you will ask for, and how much you are hoping to get. Because you like a bit of competition, consider using your own gift to challenge your prospects to give more. You might even consider telling a donor that you're willing to raise your own gift if they'll match it.

But remember, although you go into each meeting with a clear intention, you also have the ability to be flexible and responsive to your donor. Use that ability to change your ask if another figure seems more appropriate while you're with the donor.

Rainmakers and the Five-Part Ask

A well-designed ask usually has five parts, and you might want to think about and review each of these before you begin your solicitation.

Introduction

This early portion of a meeting gives you a chance to focus the attention of your donor, and to find common ground through discussion of everyday topics. As an extrovert, you'll probably find this part of the visit easy and comfortable.

Dialogue

This important portion of the ask relies on your ability to pose open-ended questions that draw your prospect into a discussion related to your organization. Prepare some questions in advance, but then let your love of interaction guide you to questions that are triggered by your donor's interests.

Presentation

Don't let an extrovert's enthusiasm for talking lead you astray at this point in the visit. Your presentation should take *no more than three minutes.* Rely on the facts and figures you are so good at synthesizing, along with a focus on your organization's goals and outcomes, to ensure that less is more in your presentation.

Asking for a Gift

◆ Come to the meeting with objectives in mind.

◆ Consider challenging your donor to help you reach the goal, or to match your own gift.

◆ Rely on your natural instincts as a closer.

 practical tip

Ask

The ask is the one sentence you should memorize in advance: "Would you consider making a gift of $_____ to this project?" Trust your judgment of the dollar amount, even if it's not what you planned in advance. And be sure to *wait for your donor to respond* before you move into the close.

Close

As a Rainmaker, you will be happy to close a gift. While you enjoy the process of interacting with donors, few things make you happier than reaching an agreement and tying down all the loose ends. It's not your nature to let a donor meeting end without specifying amounts, payment schedules, and next steps. Even if your donors decide not to make a gift, you're likely to find ways to involve them in some aspect of the organization and plan to go back to them when they're ready to give.

How a Rainmaker Follows Through

Of course, getting the gift is just one more step in a process that doesn't end when the amount has been agreed upon. You'll want to follow up immediately to thank the donor and confirm the gift, making sure there is no confusion or misunderstanding.

If you are working with development staff members, be sure to report to them as soon as possible so that they can send the official follow-up response and thank-you.

Be sure to follow up in person. You can do this with email or more formal written correspondence. And because many of the people you ask are likely to be friends or acquaintances, you'll want to find ways for the people who make commitments to become engaged with your organization. You understand very well the long-term strategic benefit of using every opportunity to draw them close.

Your ability to be strategic and patient in building strong relationships will be put to great use during this post-ask period.

❏ Read Chapters Three, Five, and Six to better understand Kindred Spirits, Mission Controllers, and Go-Getters.

❏ Write down three ways that you could work more effectively with colleagues who have each Asking Style.

❏ Make a list of the six people with whom you work most closely. What do you think their Asking Styles are?

❏ Spend some time with each of these people, talking about your style and theirs.

❏ Identify three ways that your colleagues' styles complement each other and three things that are likely to rub one or both of you the wrong way.

❏ If you're working with a few specific donors, write down what you believe their styles to be, and list three things that you will do to accommodate each of their styles.

to-do lists

To Recap

◆ Rainmakers are analytic extroverts. They are comfortable with people, and able to succeed with a wide range of donors.

◆ Rainmakers approach asking with patience, flexibility, courage, and persistence. They relish asking for significant gifts, and are able to solicit their personal contacts.

◆ They like to be thoroughly prepared, which means armed with specifics.

◆ Because they are strategic and patient, Rainmakers understand the importance of building long-term relationships.

Chapter Five

How Mission Controllers Ask

IN THIS CHAPTER

- ···→ Understanding Mission Controllers

- ···→ How Mission Controllers select prospects, get ready to ask, set up the meeting, ask for the gift, and follow through

- ···→ Practical tips for Mission Controllers

andra M., the director of a large regional hospital, is a Mission Controller. She is a gifted analyst and has built a strong development team by being well organized and thorough. She makes a point of being well prepared, and hates flying by the seat of her pants.

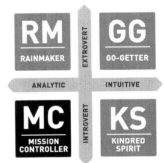

While Sandra is not the most inspiring speaker, and doesn't push herself forward in a group, other people listen to what she has to say. That's because they rely on her to be clear, accurate, and logical. Sandra doesn't make decisions quickly, but once she's made them, she's doesn't like to change her mind.

As a Mission Controller, Sandra is generally more comfortable with corporate and foundation fundraising than she is with individuals. But asking people for gifts is most definitely part of Sandra's job, and she's built a great team of fundraising professionals who help her succeed.

Sandra is similar to other Mission Controllers, who epitomize the expression "still waters run deep." Thoughtful and private, Mission Controllers are often "the smartest people in the room," and, though they can sometimes be maddeningly literal—at least in the view of their intuitive colleagues—they command the loyalty of their "flashier" peers because they themselves are unwaveringly loyal.

Mission Controllers can also be the most conscientious, most reliable, and most steadfast people on any team. They shine with donors who value and appreciate their extensive knowledge, thoughtful approach, and quiet strength of character.

If, like Sandra, you are a Mission Controller (analytic and introverted), you will probably:

◆ Be organized, methodical, and detailed

◆ Base decisions on information and analysis

◆ Be private and quietly thoughtful

◆ Require detailed information

◆ Connect with donors through your thoroughness and logic

Selecting Who to Ask

◆ Corporate or foundation donors are natural prospects for a Mission Controller.

◆ You are also willing to help with any other priority donors, including those who've been overlooked by others.

◆ Organization comes naturally to you, and you can select and pursue multiple donors at a time.

practical tip

Let's look at how Mission Controllers function as solicitors.

How a Mission Controller Selects Who to Ask

If you're a Mission Controller, you might be slightly uncomfortable about the idea of asking for gifts. But if that's one of your responsibilities, you will approach the task with characteristic care, and when you have mastered the information you need, you will be willing to speak with anyone.

Because your approach to most things is based on your mastery of detail, you are ideally suited to soliciting corporations and foundations. These organizations typically require just the kind of information you excel at delivering. However, you needn't limit yourself to institutional asks. Because you are willing to do what needs to be done, select those prospects who really *should* be seen but have, for some reason, been neglected by others.

Like your analytical "cousins," the Rainmakers, you have the courage to ask a wide range of people for gifts, though, in your case, that courage is motivated by a sense of duty, not competitiveness. You are able to ask friends or relatives, high-dollar donors, and donors who just should be seen because they've been giving year after year. You will even be willing, if not comfortable, to ask people who are new to your organization, because you know that this job needs to be done.

Since you are well organized and good at following through, you can pursue many donors simultaneously. A spreadsheet of who you have contacted, what the next steps are, and the eventual results of your asks will help you manage the process effectively, and is just the kind of approach you thrive on.

How a Mission Controller Gets Ready to Ask

If you're a Mission Controller, "preparation" is your middle name. You wouldn't dream of asking someone for a gift if you hadn't done your homework—and done it well. You'll want to review the budget, the annual report, the strategic plan, and any other documents that outline your organization's history and plans.

Of course, you'll also want to gather as much information as you can about your prospective donor. Determine the amount you will ask for based on your research. And prepare some questions to draw the donor out, such as:

Getting Ready to Ask

◆ Take the time you need to prepare thoroughly.

◆ Bring questions to get the conversation going.

◆ Assemble a full packet of material to guide you through the solicitation, and a copy to give your donor.

 practical tip

◆ "Why are you a donor to this organization?"

◆ "How did you get connected to this organization?"

◆ "Have you been to see our program recently?"

You might find it helpful to put together a detailed outline of how you plan to solicit the gift, including a written statement of your presentation. You are not likely to feel well prepared unless you have written documents on hand that show the facts of the organization, how it has grown, who it serves, and what the fundraising will make possible. Bring a copy of this material for your reference, and an additional copy to leave with your donors.

Finally, because of your emphasis on training and professionalism, consider getting solicitation training. You will feel more confident, and enjoy your donor visits more, if you are fully prepared and versed in the best practices of the field.

How a Mission Controller Sets Up the Meeting

While a Rainmaker or a Go-Getter would be comfortable picking up the phone to schedule a meeting, you are likely to prefer to send a letter (by email or the old-fashioned way) to introduce the subject of a visit to your donor.

Because you probably believe that every donor will want the same amount of information you would want, you will feel more comfortable sending material in advance for the donor to review. Then you will follow up with an email or a phone call to schedule the meeting.

Be sure you are prepared with the answer to the question, "Why should we meet? Can't we just take care of this on the phone?"

Setting Up the Meeting

◆ Send your donors a letter letting them know that you will be calling to schedule a meeting.

◆ Include the information that you would want if you were the donor.

◆ Be prepared to explain why meeting in person is essential.

 practical tip

Your answer might be that you think it is important to meet in person so that you can lay out a fully-developed case rather than have only a few minutes on the phone. We have ample evidence that meeting in person leads to a richer conversation and that personal visits are likely to result in larger gifts. Meeting people in person will give you the opportunity to get to know your donors better. You'll be able to see how they live, connect with them personally, and get a much clearer sense of how you might engage them. So hold firm on the idea of meeting in person.

How a Mission Controller Asks for a Gift

As a Mission Controller, you are a very effective solicitor. You have the patience to ask questions of a donor and then sit back and listen to their answers.

Like a Kindred Spirit, your quiet style gives donors plenty of room to be an active part of the solicitation process, in effect talking themselves into a gift. And while you don't light up the room the way a Go-Getter does, the case you make will be well prepared and cogent.

> ### Asking for a Gift
>
> ◆ Preparation and your natural sense of duty will help you move through any awkwardness you may feel.
>
> ◆ Monitor your donor's reactions to make sure you're not giving too much information.
>
> ◆ Push yourself to make the ask; then you can relax and close.
>
> practical tip

Your thoroughness and full mastery of details enables donors to feel confident in the effectiveness of the organization you represent. And, since you'll almost certainly be prepared to answer whatever questions your donor asks, your responses will further deepen the donor's understanding of your organization.

Mission Controllers and the Five-Part Ask

A well-designed ask usually has five parts. You might want to think about and review each of these before you begin your solicitation.

Introduction

This early portion of a meeting gives you a chance to focus the attention of your donor and find common ground through discussion of everyday topics. As an introvert, getting started might be the most challenging part of the conversation. One technique for overcoming this discomfort is to focus internally on your sense of duty rather than on any personal discomfort you might feel.

Dialogue

This most important part of the ask relies on your ability to pose open-ended questions that draw the prospect into a discussion about the value of your organization. The questions that you have prepared in advance will guide you through this portion of the visit. Be sure to adjust the order of questions to respond to what your donor has said, rather than proceeding from one question to the next in pre-determined order.

Presentation

Remember that a presentation doesn't need to be exhaustive to be effective. As you deliver the comments you have prepared, be alert to signs of restlessness; these might indicate that your donor has less interest in detail than you do. If you are in doubt about your donor's reaction, simply ask if your donor wants to hear more.

Ask

The ask itself is the one sentence that should be memorized in advance: "Would you consider making a gift of $_____to this project?" Be confident in the research you've done and ask for the amount you decided on. Then wait for the donor's response before you move into the close.

Close

While you might find closing slightly awkward, rely once again on your preparation. Once your donor has made a commitment, you can return to the morc comfortable ground of reviewing and clarifying logistical details. If your donor needs more time to decide, just clarify the specific next steps in the process. For example, you might suggest that the donor visit your programs or meet with your board chair. As a Mission Controller, you understand people who don't make decisions quickly. And if your donor says "no," be sure to learn everything you can about their decision and explore other ways your donor might want to be involved.

How a Mission Controller Follows Through

Of course, getting the gift is just one more step in a process that doesn't end when you and the donor come to an agreement. As a detail-oriented Mission Controller, you'll find it natural to immediately clarify the terms, details, and purpose of a gift, so there's no confusion later.

If you are working with a development staff, be sure to report to them as soon as possible so that they can send the organization's official follow-up response and thank-you. You'll also want to follow up personally with your donor. You can do this with an email thank-you, followed by a more formal written correspondence.

If your donors include people who *should* be asked but have previously been neglected by the organization, let them know how much their gift is valued.

❏ Read Chapters Three, Four and Six to better understand Kindred Spirits, Rainmakers, and Go-Getters.

❏ Write down three ways that you could work more effectively with colleagues who have each Asking Style.

❏ Make a list of the six people with whom you work most closely. What do you think their Asking Styles are?

❏ Spend some time with each of these people, talking about your style and theirs.

❏ Identify three ways that your styles complement each other and three things that are likely to rub one or both of you the wrong way.

❏ If you're working with a few specific donors, write down what you believe their styles to be, and list three things that you will do to accommodate each of their styles.

Be specific about what it will achieve. And develop an action plan that you or your colleagues can follow, over time, to draw new donors closer to your organization.

To Recap

◆ Mission Controllers are analytic introverts who care about, and rely on, their mastery of detail.

◆ Mission Controllers approach asking with thoroughness, reliability, and analytic intelligence. They are able to succeed with donors of all sorts.

◆ Mission Controllers function best when they are thoroughly versed in the history and facts of a case. They should prepare and study written documents, and send them to their donors in advance.

◆ Following up on details and letting donors know how their gifts are being used, specifically, are Mission Controller strengths.

Chapter Six

How Go-Getters Ask

IN THIS CHAPTER

···→ Understanding Go-Getters

···→ How Go-Getters select prospects, get ready to ask, set up the meeting, ask for the gift, and follow through

···→ Practical tips for Go-Getters

Marianna H. is a Go-Getter. The development director for a social justice organization, she's energetic, charismatic, and always has a smile on her face. Marianna will tell you, with a twinkle in her eye, that she gets people to "fall under her spell." And in reality, that's just what they do. She's outgoing and exciting to listen to, and people believe what she says even when she doesn't back it up with facts and figures. Marianna's strong suit—one of several—is the courage to articulate big ideas. She can set forth challenging goals in a way that makes other people believe that her vision can be achieved and then want to help her achieve it.

Since Marianna knows that planning and details are not her strengths, she usually makes sure to work with people whose skill sets complement her own, and she always gives them ample credit for their contribution to success.

Marianna is a natural-born collaborator, as are many Go-Getters. Her flexible style encourages her to ask other people for advice, and she adapts, based on their feedback, in ways that make her even more successful.

This fluidity is both a source of power and of challenge for Go-Getters like Marianna. They are wonderful at inspiring and involving others. But, unlike their extroverted "cousins," the Rainmakers, they are happier when they're exploring options than they are with the finality of tying down a gift.

Fortunately, this lack of interest in closure doesn't compromise a Go-Getter's success. With their outgoing personalities and personal empathy, Go-Getters make excellent fundraisers. Highly aware of their strengths and limits, Go-Getters often choose to work with people of other styles so that they can focus on big-picture goals, and leave the small executional details to others.

If you, like Marianna, are a Go-Getter (extroverted and intuitive), you're probably:

- ◆ Enthusiastic, creative, and flexible

- ◆ Someone who thrives on high-energy experience

- ◆ Happy as the center of attention

- ◆ A big-picture thinker

- ◆ Undeterred by anxiety—it doesn't stop you from taking action

Let's look at how Go-Getters function as solicitors.

How a Go-Getter Selects Who to Ask

People see Go-Getters as courageous, but they don't realize that the Go-Getters are *having fun*. As a Go-Getter, you enjoy talking with people. You're a junkie for fluid conversations about shared values that inspire a sense of connectedness. And you're good at making that kind of conversation happen. This ability uniquely qualifies you to ask donors for gifts—because, at its heart, the fundraising process is really a conversation that connects people over shared values!

Because Go-Getters aren't interested in managing complex processes, you might find it easier to pick only two or three prospects at a time, and wait until they close before you take on more. You'll find the management side of soliciting less onerous when you keep it well contained and focus on building individual relationships.

Go-Getters can and should select prospects who they believe have (a) the ability to give and (b) a reason to do so. You will be comfortable selecting family and friends, or even people you don't yet know. In your enthusiasm for reaching out to people, don't forget that your prospects should be qualified.

Sometimes, as a Go-Getter, you will get so engaged in the process of talking with people about your organization that you lose sight of your primary goal: to raise money! So be careful to spend your time wisely and select prospects who have the ability to make significant gifts or open important doors.

Selecting People to Ask

◆ Select prospects who have the ability to give and a reason to do so.

◆ Take just a couple prospects at a time; then go back for more when those have closed.

◆ Pick some prospects who are not yet close to your organization. This is a good challenge for you.

◆ Don't forget that your goal is *to raise money!*

practical tip

How a Go-Getter Gets Ready to Ask

If you're a Go-Getter, you're well aware that facts, figures, and details are not your natural friends. You'd much rather grab a few big ideas and run with them.

This is not a failing; it's the way you function best. So when you're getting ready to ask, you should do what you do best. Grab the big ideas and summarize them for yourself, into a few simple bullet points. Then find someone—a colleague, a friend, or even your mirror!—and practice talking through those points. Find the words and the language that resonate for you, making sure that you clearly express each nuance of the points you want to make.

Getting Ready to Ask

◆ Rely on big ideas as the way to make your case.

◆ Be sure to have a fact sheet you can pull out if your prospect asks for data.

◆ Gather a couple of real-life stories that you can share with prospective donors.

◆ Let your donors fall under *your organization's* spell by sharing the aspects that are close to their hearts.

practical tip

Put together a page of salient facts—things that your donors are likely to ask—and be sure to keep it with you. No need to memorize it. If you're talking to someone who wants "just the facts, ma'am," pull out that sheet, and you can deliver.

You might also spend some time unearthing true stories that communicate the mission of your organization. Spend a bit of time with program directors, or even in the field, and find the stories that give you goose bumps. These stories are likely to come in handy when you talk with other people about your organization.

Spend a bit of time getting to know your prospective donors before you go to see them. Learn enough about them to enable you to discuss how they relate to your organization, and prepare some questions that will help you take the conversation about their interests to a deeper level.

Remember that, while you have the capacity to bring people "under your spell," this process is not really about *you*. What you really want to do is *get donors to share* the heart of their own interests. In fact, the true magic of fundraising, for Go-Getters, is that—when you give your donors the time and space to share—you'll help them fall under the spell of *their own desire* to support your organization.

How a Go-Getter Sets Up the Meeting

As a Go-Getter, the telephone is your friend. Even in a phone call, you are hard to turn down. So while you may use email to get the conversation going, if your donor is being elusive, try the phone to get a date on someone's calendar.

Be sure you are prepared to answer the question, "Why should we meet? Can't we just take care of this on the phone?" As an extrovert, you learn by talking, so you might want to try out various responses to this question by role playing with a colleague or friend. Remember that when you meet people in person, you'll get to know them better. You'll be able to see how they live, use your magnetism to connect with them personally, and get a much clearer sense of how you might engage them.

> ### Setting Up the Meeting
>
> ◆ Contact donors by phone to schedule your meetings.
>
> ◆ Practice dealing with resistance by role playing with a friend or colleague.
>
> ◆ Make calls to schedule meetings when the moment feels right, rather than schedule blocks of time to make those calls.
>
> practical tip

Go-Getters are inclined to grab the moment. So rather than work through a long list of contacts, pick people to call when the spirit moves you. (Be sure, however, that you keep good records, and set out some goals to keep you on track!)

How a Go-Getter Asks for a Gift

Go-Getters are flexible and cooperative, and you can use those skills when you solicit gifts. You might go into a donor visit with several possible gift levels in mind, and be fully comfortable about deciding what to ask for as you are talking to the donor. This works because, unlike some of your colleagues with different styles, you are intuitively able to "read" your donor and adapt your ask based on the donor's cues.

Just be sure you ask for *a specific amount*. As already noted, Go-Getters have a natural fascination with *process*, rather than outcomes, and that might lead you to forget to ask at all! Don't let your avid curiosity about every aspect of your donor's life, history, thoughts, and feelings distract you from the purpose of your visit. Instead, use the closeness you have established to help your donor commit to a gift!

Asking for a Gift

◆ Come to the meeting with clear objectives in mind, including several dollar amounts you might ask for depending on how things go.

◆ Don't use a script. Rely instead on your natural ability— augmented by role-play and practice!—to articulate a big, compelling case.

◆ Consider bringing a partner to help you close the gift, if you think you'll hesitate.

 practical tip

Go-Getters and the Five-Part Ask

A well-designed ask usually has five parts, and you might want to think about and review each of these before you begin your solicitation.

Introduction

This early portion of a meeting gives you a chance to focus the attention of your donor and find common ground through discussion of everyday topics. As an extrovert, this is easy and comfortable for you.

Dialogue

This most important part of the ask relies on your ability to pose open-ended questions that draw your prospect into a discussion related to your organization. You might want to prepare some questions in advance—though, as an extrovert, you are likely to be able to craft questions on the spot that are triggered by interests your prospect expresses.

Presentation

Go-Getters stand out for their ability to make the case in a way that makes people tingle. For you, it's not about the budget, the programs, or any other specifics. For you, the heart of the case is the long-term impact your organization will have on the community and the broader world. This focus on making a real difference is a powerful case that many people cannot make convincingly, because they get tangled up "in the weeds" of detail, and the specific needs of their organization. Go-Getters have a special talent for presenting big and compelling ideas. *Just remember to give your donor time to ask questions* so that the donor can visualize being part of the picture you're presenting, and can ask for any necessary facts or supplementary information.

Ask

The ask is the one sentence you should memorize in advance: "Would you consider making a gift of $_____to this project?" As a Go-Getter, although you should have an amount in mind before your visit, you can feel confident about altering that amount based on your interaction with the donor. Once you've made the ask, discipline yourself to *wait for your donor to respond*, and before you move into the close.

Close

Because of your love for open-ended discussions, this is the biggest challenge for you. Most donors are comfortable putting off a decision, and if you give them "wiggle room," the gift you seek might never get made. *So make yourself tie down the specifics*—and if that means inviting someone else to come help you close, be sure to take that person to your meeting! You're much too adept at the asking process to lose it all at this critical stage. Should your donor need more time to decide, don't just leave the conversation open; tie down specific next steps. If your donor declines to make a gift, find out if there are other ways your donor might like to get more involved.

Following Through

◆ Indulge your natural inclination to do more than just write a standard thank-you. You might have fun thinking of something special.

◆ Be sure that the standard formal response to a gift is also sent in a timely way.

◆ Follow up with persons who say "no" to make sure they feel fine about their response, and explore other opportunities that your relationship might afford.

practical tip

How a Go-Getter Follows Through

You are likely a person of large gestures, and you might want to follow a generous gift with something more than a simple thank-you note. For you, traditional follow-up doesn't ring true, so consider sending something special. You might send flowers or a photo you took of the donor when you visited. Or you might send a photo of someone whose life was changed because of a gift. Or how about a book you think the donor might like? At the very least, you will want to write a personal note letting the donor know just how much the gift means to you, as well as to your organization.

Of course, every gift needs a formal response that thanks the donor, reiterates the specifics, and gives the donor a tax receipt. Be sure that you communicate to staff members clearly so that they can handle paperwork within a couple of days of the gift. This isn't particularly exciting for you, and will be easy to neglect if you don't pay attention. But pay attention, because it's critical.

❑ Read Chapters Three through Five to better understand Kindred Spirits, Rainmakers, and Mission Controllers. Write down three ways that you could work more effectively with colleagues who have each Asking Style.

❑ Make a list of the six people with whom you work most closely. What do you think their Asking Styles are?

❑ Spend some time with each of these people, talking about your style and theirs.

❑ Identify three ways that your styles complement each other and three things that are likely to rub one or both of you the wrong way.

❑ If you're working with a few specific donors, write down what you believe their styles to be, and list three things that you will do to accommodate each of their styles.

Because you are a Go-Getter, you will also be inclined to take care of the donor who has decided *not* to give. While hearing "no" rocks some people back on their heels, you're more likely to want to explore other opportunities when someone says "no" to a gift. And you might even worry about the effect of that "no" on *the donor*. In either case, you might wish to follow up with the donor.

To Recap

◆ Go-Getters are intuitive extroverts whose charismatic style can inspire others. They are particularly successful when they focus their attention on donors who have the ability to give, and a reason to do so.

◆ Go-Getters approach asking with creativity, charisma, passion, and flexibility. They are impatient with details, and want their donors to fall "under the spell" of a big vision.

◆ They are strongest when they can "seize the moment" and follow their passions instead of a pre-set plan.

◆ As natural collaborators, they work well with people of other styles—particularly those who thrive on the details Go-Getters find boring.

Chapter Seven

When Asking Styles Work Together

IN THIS CHAPTER

···→ Why we're drawn to people who share our Asking Style

···→ The challenges and advantages of partnering with people of different styles

···→ The challenges and advantages of partnering with people who share our own style

···→ How to make every style pairing work

You might think that the best way to manage people's Asking Styles would be to put people with the same styles together on a team—or to have fundraisers solicit donors with the same styles.

Using this approach, Kindred Spirits would solicit only those donors who were Kindred Spirits. Rainmakers would always mentor or supervise other Rainmakers.

Does that plan sound good to you?

Or does it sound stilted, boring, and even counterproductive?

If the latter, congratulations: you've grasped an important point about Asking Styles, which is that they exist to facilitate *inclusion*, not *exclusion*.

Don't Put All Your Eggs in One Style Basket

It's natural that, as human beings, we're drawn to spend time and connect with people who share our way of being in the world. Often, with people who share our styles, we feel a sense of ease and camaraderie that's natural and satisfying.

Similarly, you might find it comfortable to work with people who share your style. Common approaches and shared assumptions might make those relationships easy, too.

Yet something critically important is lost when we interact *only* with those who share our Asking Styles—when we build our soliciting careers, or manage our organizations, along lines of style compatibility.

As you know, the four different Asking Styles are defined by combining two uniquely valuable ways of gathering information, and two uniquely valuable ways of interacting with the world.

How Many Board Members Does It Take To...?

The vice president of a small college once asked me to figure out why the college's board seemed stuck in "analysis paralysis." It turned out that eighteen of the twenty board members were Mission Controllers. This imbalance meant that no one was watching the big picture (Mission Controllers are past-oriented, not focused on future possibilities), and that planning meetings were focused on what had gone wrong, rather than shaping a vision of what might be.

The failure of this board eventually led to the demise of the college's president—a strong Mission Controller who had appointed most of its members. Intentionally or not, he'd created the board in his own image, forgetting that, without a diversity of styles and thinking, there can be no lively debate or forward movement.

stories from
the real world

The two ways of gathering information are:

◆ *Analytic*: A precise, past- and present-focused approach

◆ *Intuitive*: A big picture, possibilities-oriented approach

The two ways of interacting with the world are:

◆ *Extrovert*: An outward-focused, more gregarious approach

◆ *Introvert*: An inward-focused, more reflective approach

EXTROVERT

ANALYTIC   INTUITIVE

INTROVERT

You can probably imagine many situations in which it would be good to have someone with each of these qualities on your team. So *why would you restrict yourself, your team, or your donors to only two of these four* Asking Style characteristics? Because that's just what happens when two people with the same Asking Style are paired together!

When Opposite Asking Styles Work Together

There are two Asking Style combinations that give you the benefit of all four capacities discussed above. They are:

Rainmaker + Kindred Spirit

Go-Getter + Mission Controller

Each of these pairings provides introversion, extroversion, analysis, and intuition.

What's interesting, though, is that—useful as these matchups can be—the two people who are paired together can find it hard to combine their strengths. A look at each style's typical characteristics shows why this is often the case.

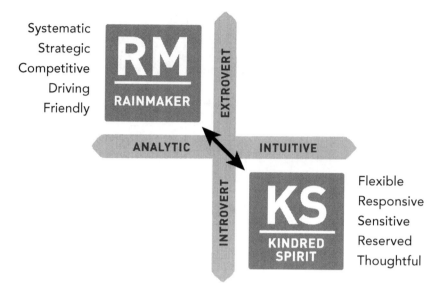

When Rainmakers are matched with Kindred Spirits, their styles can infuriate each other:

◆ A Kindred Spirit's intense focus on emotions (the asker's own and other people's) might strike a Rainmaker as a waste of time—or even as whiny self-indulgence.

◆ A Rainmaker's "take no prisoners" attitude might strike a Kindred Spirit as aggressive—or worse, egotistical and cruel.

◆ The Kindred Spirit's intuitive approach to an ask ("Let's play it by ear when we see what the donor is feeling") could inspire the well-prepared Rainmaker's disdain.

◆ The Rainmaker's reliance on a strategy (and insistence that everyone follow it) could move the creative Kindred Spirit to despair.

And so on, down through their respective lists of traits.

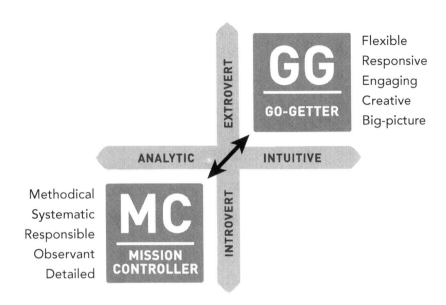

The same sort of frustrations and misunderstandings can plague Go-Getters and Mission Controllers when they pair up:

◆ A Go-Getter's "flexibility" might strike a Mission Controller as careless—or worse, as playing fast and loose with the facts.

◆ A Mission Controller's cautious speech might strike a Go-Getter (whose brain moves at one hundred miles per hour) as sluggishness—or worse, as stupidity.

◆ The Go-Getter's charisma, vision, and charm might inspire wariness and suspicion in the Mission Controller.

◆ The Mission Controller's insistence on detail and specificity might put the Go-Getter to sleep.

Working across Asking Styles takes patience, perception, and perseverance. Fortunately, these are the qualities that will make you a successful fundraiser, whatever your style!

principle

So Why Bother Mixing Styles (and How)?

Given the difficulty of cross-style communication, it's no wonder that many people throw up their hands and stick to partnering with the colleagues who are most like themselves.

And that's too bad—because pairing with colleagues who are *different* from us is one of the best ways we can grow. (And we haven't even gotten to the benefits inherent when "cross-style" partners interact with donors!)

So, what do you do when fate, or curiosity, or your development director pairs you with someone whose Asking Style is different from your own?

◆ *Talk things over.* Tell each other about the strengths and weaknesses of your individual Asking Styles, and discuss the areas where your styles differ.

◆ *Identify potential trouble spots.* If you need quiet time to reflect, but your colleague doesn't work well in silence, note this as an area of possible difficulty.

◆ *Develop strategies* for capturing the benefits that come with difference, while avoiding possible pitfalls. If the two of you are going on a donor call, how will you decide who takes the lead when you don't yet know the donor's style? Will you present very different types of cases for support? How will you divide the material so that you're not playing tug-of-war?

Cross-style partners can be among the most successful fundraising teams. When Joe, a Kindred Spirit, pairs up with Yumi, a Rainmaker, Yumi knows that Joe's compassion will touch their donor's heart, and Joe relies on Yumi to ask for a stretch gift (and usually get it).

Similarly, Adrianna, a Go-Getter, loves visiting prospects with her Mission Controller colleague Pamela. Adrianna can relax and charm their donor, secure in the knowledge that Pamela will keep the interaction, and the ask, on solid ground.

 practical tip

When Similar Asking Styles Work Together

Just as pairing up with someone of another Asking Style can create new types of challenges, so can pairing up with someone of your *own* style. Both of you can be lulled into the false sense of comfort that comes from seeing things from a similar perspective—only to discover that your point of view might not be shared by a donor with a different style.

It's also common for solicitors who share the same style or style characteristics to feel that something is *missing* from the mix. A Mission Controller might miss the energy that a Go-Getter or Rainmaker would bring; a Go-Getter might miss the focus on closing that a Rainmaker or Mission Controller contributes.

There are also active "watch-outs" to consider with same-style pairings. Here are the most common pitfalls that beset same-style solicitor pairs, and how to avoid them:

◆ *Two extroverts can hog the limelight.* When two Rainmakers, two Go-Getters, or a Rainmaker and a Go-Getter go out to ask, decide in advance who's going to take the lead. You're both talkers, and without carefully assigning roles, you could end up overpowering an introverted donor, or competing with an extroverted donor who also wants to get a word in!

◆ *Two introverts can sit in silence.* When two Kindred Spirits, two Mission Controllers, or a Kindred Spirit and a Mission Controller go out to ask, decide in advance who's going to lead. You're both skilled listeners, but someone has to present the case!

◆ *Two analytics can leave a donor feeling cold.* Facts and figures fascinate analytics, but not every donor finds them compelling. When two Rainmakers, two Mission Controllers, or a Rainmaker and a Mission Controller go out to ask, be sure to practice some inspiring stories, and decide which one of you will tell them.

◆ *Two intuitives can leave a donor unconvinced.* Stories and big picture ideas are not a sufficient case for many donors. When two Kindred Spirits, two Go-Getters, or a Kindred Spirit and a Go-Getter go out to ask, be prepared with facts and figures that supplement your inspiring stories.

watch out!

Every partnership has challenges, but all of them share the same set of solutions. Take these steps whenever you find yourself paired with another fundraiser:

❑ *Review* the Asking Styles, with a focus on how each of the other three is similar to and different from your own.

❑ *Communicate* with your asking partner about the strengths and limits of each of your styles.

❑ *Anticipate* possible problem areas, and talk about how you will handle them.

❑ *Coordinate* your skills and strengths, so that you, your organization, and your donors will benefit.

To Recap

◆ When solicitors of the same style work together, their combined skills are limited to two out of four possibilities.

◆ Two combinations of styles encompass all four skills (introversion, extroversion, analytics, and intuition): Rainmakers plus Kindred Spirits, and Mission Controllers plus Go-Getters.

◆ Two extroverts on an ask should guard against competing with each other or with the donor.

◆ Two introverts on an ask should guard against silence, or a leadership vacuum.

◆ Two analytics on an ask should guard against neglecting to inspire their donor or present the big picture.

◆ Two intuitives on an ask should guard against making a vague, unconvincing case.

Chapter Eight

How to Solicit with Asking Styles

IN THIS CHAPTER

···→ The role of executive directors and development directors

···→ Ideal assignments for each Asking Style

···→ How to read and respond to your donor's style

In today's nonprofit world, *everyone* needs to know about Asking Styles. Executive directors and development directors can use this knowledge to match donors with solicitors, and to manage the diversity of styles on their board and staff.

Staff members need to understand their donors' diverse styles, and the styles of colleagues they sometimes team up with to make an ask.

Board members will function more effectively when they understand their own styles and those of the board as a whole, their board colleagues, and the organization's staff. (For more on how a *board* can have an Asking Style, see the Stories from the Real World sidebar on page 56 in Chapter Seven.)

The Buck Stops Here: When You're the Boss

Although *every* person in the fundraising world has a complex and challenging job, no one carries more roles than executive and development directors.

❑ Be sure that everyone on your staff is familiar with *their own* Asking Style. It doesn't help to know a donor's style if you aren't familiar and comfortable with your own.

❑ Talk to your team members about the various Asking Style combinations discussed at length in Chapter Seven.

❑ Before a volunteer or staff member goes on a visit, share your thoughts about the donor's style, just as you would share insights about that donor's interests, background, and giving priorities.

to-do lists

Yet there is another role that, if you're willing to play it, might lighten the others. We'll call it "Coordinator of Asking Styles."

The role is yours because you're ideally positioned to match donors with the right solicitors, create effective cross-style asking teams, and help your board be more effective. These measures can greatly enhance your organization's impact—all through your knowledge of Asking Styles.

Of course, the reality is that your time isn't endless, while the list of tasks on your plate always seems to be. But a working knowledge of Asking Styles can help you meet your many obligations with less frustration and wasted time.

In Chapter Seven, I talked about the advantages of cross-style teams, and also flagged some of the most common pitfalls of cross-style *and* same-style solicitations:

On the one hand, cross-style pairings make your teams more able to respond to your donors' needs, and to be maximally flexible in the ask. On the other, it's just not always possible to send two people out on a call, let alone two people who both know the donor and have an optimal mix of Asking Styles. Because we don't have full control of the circumstances, we often end up with unlikely or not ideal pairings—when we're able to make pairings at all!

So what can an executive director or development director do?

Plenty!

Help your solicitors prepare—both mentally, and with materials—for the areas in which their style might not be compatible with the donor's style. And if they're going to solicit in a pair, be sure that both people understand the challenges, as well as the advantages, of matching their Asking Styles.

Understanding what each person brings to the table and discussing it before the solicitation gives your solicitors the biggest edge—whether you're sending out one solicitor or two, and whatever their individual Asking Styles.

That said, here are some specific ideas about who to assign to each Asking Style, when possible:

Kindred Spirits

Kindred Spirits tend to take rejection personally, and consequently, they don't want to risk creating a rift in close personal relationships by asking for gifts. They do best with prospects they're not as close to, but with whom they share a passion for your organization.

For these reasons, assign former donors and others who are already passionate about your organization (that is, people with whom they're likely to succeed) to your Kindred Spirit solicitors.

Rainmakers

Rainmakers are relatively fearless, goal-oriented, and good closers. They are able to accept rejection without experiencing it as a personal affront, and they like asking for big numbers. For these reasons, assign your high-level prospects to them.

Rainmakers also find it easier than many other styles to solicit people they are close to. And since Rainmakers tend to be systematic, they might be able to manage more prospects at one time than some of the other styles could handle.

Mission Controllers

Mission Controllers, like Rainmakers, are information and systems people. You can rely on them to make serious, well-prepared presentations, and they shine in situations where thoroughness and a serious approach are valued.

One Note of Caution

Does all of this mean that you shouldn't assign your highest-level donor to a Kindred Spirit, or that Go-Getters can't present factual data?

Of course not! The top rule of fundraising is to know who you're dealing with—and that means your staff, as well as your donors.

But in a situation with unknowns, or if your staff is less experienced, or if you can choose from among several solicitors, your knowledge of Asking Styles can help you build your staff's skills, confidence, and success.

important

For these reasons, assign business, foundation, or corporate donors who expect fully-developed presentations to your Mission Controllers.

Go-Getters

Go-Getters have a compelling energy that is contagious. They are relatively comfortable making contact with prospective donors, and have a talent for drawing people in.

For these reasons, assign the prospects you want to bring closer to your organization (including new donors and those whose potential has not yet been fully engaged) to your Go-Getter solicitors.

When You're the Solicitor: Reading and Responding to a Donor's Style

In Chapters Three through Six you learned, in depth, about your own Asking Style.

You might have also read about the three other styles, and begun to think about them in relation to your colleagues.

But now, here comes the central challenge: *how do you use your knowledge of Asking Styles to more successfully solicit gifts?*

The following solicitation-specific tips build on the things you've learned so far about Kindred Spirits, Rainmakers, Mission Controllers, and Go-

Getters. They'll help you determine your donors' Asking Styles, and—more to the point—what to do about them.

They'll also help you feel more confident in dealing with people of *every* style, as long as you keep these cautions in mind:

◆ Behavior is a moving target. It can change based on the environment, or on the demands of a particular moment. So even if you see your donor acting in ways that seem to indicate their style, always keep an open mind until you've seen the person in more than one situation.

◆ When we measure other people's behavior, we always do so in relation to ourselves. So, if you're, let's say, a Kindred Spirit, don't assume someone else is a Rainmaker just because they're more analytic than you are. Similarly, if you're a Mission Controller, don't assume you're with a Kindred Spirit just because they express more emotion than you do.

◆ Even though you can legitimately lean toward the Asking Style of your donor, it's not possible or desirable for you to change your style past a certain point. Trying to act against your own style will cut you off from tremendous strength, and add a stilted, unnatural feel to what might otherwise have been a smooth interaction. So instead of trying to change yourself, think about the *positive* ways that your style can meet your donors' needs. And if your donors have needs you can't meet (for more data, anecdotes, spreadsheets, or an inspiring vision), recognize that fact without self-blame, and confidently offer them other resources.

On the next page, you will find a chart that will give you some tips for identifying people of different Asking Styles. As you become familiar with each style, you will find that simple behavior patterns give you clues about what someone's Asking Style might be.

The chart also offers tips for how to solicit people once you have identified their Asking Style. Keep in mind, however, that even as you adjust to accommodate someone else's style, you will want remain true to who you are.

If your donor...	...your donor might be a...	...and will want you to...
◆ Makes decisions by gathering as much information as possible ◆ Talks to different kinds of people with apparent ease ◆ Likes clear, well-documented information ◆ Is results driven	Rainmaker	◆ Send information in advance ◆ Be prepared with facts and figures ◆ Think through what's in it for the donor ◆ Be well organized and prompt ◆ Follow up clearly and immediately
◆ Makes decisions based on instinct ◆ Thrives on being with other people ◆ Brings passion to the cause ◆ Connects through high energy and charisma	Go-Getter	◆ Limit the quantity of information ◆ Focus on connections ◆ Be less formal and more spontaneous ◆ Get the donor to talk about the donor's passions ◆ Tie down the gift at the meeting if possible
◆ Makes decisions based on instinct ◆ Keeps his or her own counsel and is quietly thoughtful ◆ Brings passion to the cause ◆ Connects through deep commitment	Kindred Spirit	◆ Limit the quantity of information ◆ Share personally meaningful stories ◆ Leave ample space and time for the donor's responses ◆ Tie down the gift at the meeting, if possible
◆ Makes decisions by reviewing all of the material and gathering as much information as possible ◆ Keeps his or her own counsel and is quietly thoughtful ◆ Appreciates a wealth of information ◆ Connects by methodical evaluation	Mission Controller	◆ Send information in advance ◆ Lay out a thorough, systematic presentation ◆ Allow for methodical decision making ◆ Be precise and thorough in your follow-through

Like the assignments discussed earlier in this chapter, these rules aren't written in stone! Instead they are guidelines for your use. Try something, observe how it works, and refine your approach if you have to.

As always, the key is *understanding*. Knowing your strengths and your donor's expectations—many of which tie into Asking Styles—can help you approach each step of the process with greater confidence and ease.

To Recap

◆ Executive directors and development directors can help team members understand their own, and each other's, Asking Styles.

◆ As unofficial "coordinators of Asking Styles," executive directors and development directors can also make optimal decisions about pairing solicitors and assigning donors.

◆ While it's great to pair donors and solicitors based on Asking Styles, it's more important to move forward with the people and resources that you have.

◆ Reading and responding to a donor's presumed style is useful, but remember to be flexible in case you've misidentified the donor's style.

Chapter Nine

Boards Have Asking Styles, Too

IN THIS CHAPTER

···→ How boards develop Asking Styles

···→ The importance of diversity and balance

···→ How to explore Asking Styles with your board

···→ Asking Styles and individual board members

Boards are one of the great mysteries of fundraising. When they work, they add incalculable value and energy to an organization. When they don't, they can be dead weight, holding down the best efforts of directors and staff.

Because they're complex organisms, many people find the mystery of board success a hard one to unravel. But here's an insight that I think will help:

Boards have their own Asking Styles, just as do the people who serve on them.

Board Asking Styles evolve from a combination of these factors:

◆ *The board's composition.* Remember the small college's board in Chapter Seven, where eighteen out of twenty members shared a style? Even with a smaller plurality, one style—and its limitations—can dominate a board.

◆ *The board chair's style.* Strong leaders generally pull any organization into their comfort zones, and boards are no different. That's why having respected board members with other Asking Styles than the chair's is critical to maintaining balance.

◆ *The board's history and culture.* When a board has many Rainmakers and Mission Controllers— both analytic types that respect what's worked in the past—its history and culture can cast a long shadow. Board members might find themselves shackled by historic precedent, and forget to look for what works best today.

Getting the "Flavor" of Board Asking Styles

Think about the competitiveness of Rainmakers. The churning of ideas by Go-Getters. The emotionality of Kindred Spirits. The cautiousness of Mission Controllers.

Now think about your current board, or the boards that you've been part of—or worked with— in the past. Were any of them competitive? Idea-churning? Emotional? Cautious?

 practical tip

Similarly, a board that has a preponderance of Kindred Spirits and Go-Getters who focus on future possibilities might summarily reject the lessons of the past and "throw out the baby with the bath water."

Given all these pulls toward imbalance, you can see the potential for any board to go astray. Boards sometimes become dysfunctional because of one or more members' personal flaws. But it's also possible for a well-run board to flounder if the capabilities of one Asking Style become too dominant or extreme.

Adding to the problem is that boards are often not familiar with the concept of Asking Styles, let alone aware of the importance of seeking members who have diverse styles.

Determining the Styles on Your Board

Whether you're a board chair, a board member, or a nonprofit executive, the way to begin making your board more diverse in terms of Asking Styles is to evaluate your current members' styles.

You can do this through a group conversation or training session, or by asking each board member to read this book or take the Asking Style Assessment at www.AskingMatters.com.

When all the data has been gathered, map it out so that your entire board can view the results.

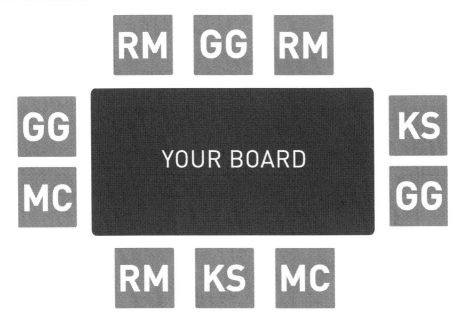

But don't stop there! You've opened the door to Asking Styles, and now it's time to start the conversation.

A discussion of the Asking Styles by people who sit on the board can generate a useful conversation about *why a board functions the way that it does.*

If your board has a preponderance of Rainmakers *or* Mission Controllers, it might have a hard time visioning, and spend more time reviewing past history than looking forward.

> Boards often look for traditional diversity (of age, race, class, gender, etc.) in new members. They look for professionals, like accountants or attorneys. And, of course, they look for individuals with financial resources and connections. But rarely does a board realize that it would also benefit from balancing itself by looking for intuitives, or introverts, or analytics, or extroverts.
>
> **observation**

If your board has mostly Go-Getters *or* Kindred Spirits, it might be a board that doesn't do enough analysis and data tracking.

Although one conversation about Asking Styles is obviously not going to fix every challenge that your board faces, it's a fantastic place to start!

Board Exercises

My background includes a lot of training, so it's natural for me to recommend a training exercise as your next step.

A training game that takes as little as thirty minutes can inspire your board and provoke ideas that create value for years to come!

And, if you don't have a good training leader in house, don't worry about execution. These exercises are quite simple to lead yourself, and you can also hire an outside trainer or consultant who's familiar with the nonprofit world. This can be a cost-effective way to get the full benefit from these exercises and your discussion of Asking Styles.

Exercise 1: Guess That Style

When all the members of your board know their own Asking Styles, ask them to guess *what the board's style is.*

After you've determined the Asking Style make up of your board, look at the answers and see how many people guessed correctly. Talk about why (or why not?) the style was obvious. If your board is competitive, give the "winners" a prize.

Exercise 2: What My Style Likes

Seat your board members in the four corners of the room, by style, and put the following questions to each group:

1. What are the characteristics that you share?

2. How can those characteristics work for you in asking for gifts?

3. What types of donors do you imagine will be the easiest and the hardest for you to solicit?

When every group has come up with their answers, have each group make a brief presentation, with flip chart.

Post all four flip charts around the room, and discuss them. How are they similar and different? What are the implications for board member effectiveness?

If one or more of the four Asking Styles are not represented on your board, talk about this gap. What capabilities would those Asking Styles bring to the group? Which of your organization's donors would appreciate or benefit from them?

Exercise 3: Let's Work Together

After going through Exercise 2, which gets people actively thinking about themselves as askers, the next natural question is, "So when are we going out to ask?"

Whether you take that next step at the same board meeting or a later one, the goal of this exercise is to get people thinking about *how they can collaborate* to ask more effectively.

Divide people into groups of mixed styles and give each group a written "donor profile." The donors might be real or imagined. The profile should include all your usual information *and* the donor's Asking Style.

Ask each group to plan a visit with this donor. Which group member (or members) will make the call, and why? How will they prepare? What fact, ideas, or stories will they present, and why? How, and when, will they make the ask?

When every group has prepared its strategy, have it report back to the whole room. Record their answers, and follow with discussion.

What Asking Styles Can Do for Your Board

A discussion of Asking Styles, and their strengths and pitfalls, often leads to a healthy debate and an increased level of self-awareness on your board. That's why exercises such as the ones above help strengthen your board, increase its flexibility, and ultimately make it more diverse. This will lead board members to think about future nominations in a more nuanced way that includes Asking Styles.

An increased awareness of Asking Styles also pays off individually. It can help people interact more smoothly, and—whether you're a board member, a board chair, or an executive who deals with the board—help you effectively support, encourage, and develop every person on your team.

Here are just a few examples of how that knowledge might be useful:

◆ If Jerry drives you crazy by going into endless detail about every topic, you might be able to call up more patience by reminding yourself before each meeting that he is a Mission Controller, and is hard-wired to use this process. (If his process bothers you, you're probably not a Mission Controller yourself!)

◆ When Joan repeatedly *throws out new ideas* for fundraising events—some of which seem off the wall—remember that, as a Go-Getter, she's getting caught up in the energy of the moment, and doesn't expect you to follow through on every idea she generates.

◆ If your board has been slow to donate money, ask Rainmaker Alexandra to *make a challenge gift.* Her competitive spirit will naturally incline her in that direction, and her gift might stimulate a higher level of giving among the rest of the board.

◆ If a meeting is getting very dry, ask Kwame, one of your board's Kindred Spirits, to share some recent stories about the mission with the rest of the group. His passion for your clients, and his natural storytelling ability, are likely to refresh everyone's energies and refocus them on your organization's mission.

In this regard, you might find it useful to include the Asking Style of each board member in your records—just as you would do with donor styles—and refresh your memory before each board meeting.

The Whole Versus the Sum of its Parts

While it's important to understand your board's overall Asking Style, the previous section demonstrates that it's also important to avoid the trap of viewing your board as *only* a whole, instead of a collection of individuals.

When we think of the board as a whole, we tend to forget that one of our primary jobs—as board members, board chairs, executives, or staff—is to treat each and every member of the board in a way that will help them function effectively in their leadership positions, and utilize their unique skills to help advance the group's effort.

And if that sounds like a lot of work, just remember how critical a well-functioning, collegial board is to your organization.

The success of your board is literally priceless—and an awareness of Asking Styles can help you achieve that success.

As in all other areas of life, we in the fundraising world do best when we treat each person individually, and build a personal relationship with each one. Identifying the Asking Style of each board member is a wonderful reminder of that fact—and a wonderful lens through which to see each person more clearly.

principle

To Recap

- ◆ Boards, like the individuals on them, have Asking Styles. An imbalance of Asking Styles on a board might create limitations or blind spots.

- ◆ Because most boards aren't aware of the importance of Asking Styles, they don't get the benefit of recruiting diverse styles.

- ◆ After assessing each member's Asking Style, bring your board together for conversations and training exercises that build an appreciation for this important area.

- ◆ Use your knowledge of Asking Styles to value each individual on your board, knowing that the results will be well worth the effort.

Closing Thoughts

You've seen the power of Asking Styles to improve the effectiveness of everyone in the fundraising business: board members, staff, executives, even donors.

But the most important place that Asking Styles can make a difference is *within you*. My hope is that knowing your own Asking Style will make you a more skilled and confident solicitor who knows that the right way to ask is *your* way.

I've seen the power of asking in my own life, in the lives of my friends, and through my work with thousands of fundraising professionals. Asking is a magic door—and if this book helps you cross the threshold, it (and I) will have done our jobs.

And an invitation...

I hope you will use the Asking Styles material in your organizations to spark conversations about asking and to help people become more comfortable asking for gifts.

If you would like presentation slides of the Asking Styles graphics, please email materials@AskingMatters.com. We will be happy to share them with you. All I ask is that you acknowledge Asking Matters®. **Asking Matters is** a project of Andrian LLC, the trademark holder of Asking Styles™.

I would love to hear your Asking Style stories. Email me at: Andrea@AskingMatters.com.

Appendix A

More Resources on Assessing Your Asking Style

The Asking Styles system was developed in conjunction with Asking Matters' innovative website at www.AskingMatters.com, dedicated to giving people the courage and information they need to ask for gifts in person.

Asking Matters provides a wide variety of material on asking, including a full thirty-question assessment to help you more accurately assess your Asking Style.

The Asking Style Assessment is based on these thirty questions designed to enable you to select one characteristic or another on each of the two axes. Because most people have characteristics in more than one of the Asking Styles, the assessment takes into account the fact that people answer these questions inconsistently. To take the Asking Style Assessment online, go to www.AskingMatters.com.

The Indicator	What it Clarifies
1. I have a good memory for facts and figures.	analytic vs. intuitive
2. I can relate easily to others.	extrovert vs. introvert
3. I often adjust my views to avoid conflict.	extrovert vs. introvert
4. I think of myself as well organized.	analytic vs. intuitive
5. My actions are usually based on systematic thinking.	analytic vs. intuitive

The Indicator	What it Clarifies
6. I act from my heart at least as often as from my head.	analytic vs. intuitive
7. I usually plan ahead.	analytic vs. intuitive
8. I am good at big-picture thinking.	analytic vs. intuitive
9. Having time alone is important to me.	extrovert vs. introvert
10. I review information thoroughly before I make decisions.	analytic vs. intuitive
11. I am curious about what makes people tick.	extrovert vs. introvert
12. I am observant of the details in my environment.	extrovert vs. introvert
13. Once I make a decision, I tend to stick with it.	analytic vs. intuitive
14. I usually form my ideas before I speak.	extrovert vs. introvert
15. I use the energy of others to help spark my thinking.	extrovert vs. introvert
16. My friends think that I "wear my heart on my sleeve."	extrovert vs. introvert
17. At a party, I don't mind introducing myself to others.	extrovert vs. introvert
18. I tend to make decisions quickly.	analytic vs. intuitive
19. I make lists and check items off when they are done.	analytic vs. intuitive
20. I prefer to work as a part of a group.	extrovert vs. introvert
21. I am happiest working on my own.	extrovert vs. introvert
22. I do most things thoroughly, from beginning to end.	analytic vs. intuitive
23. Winning is important to me.	extrovert vs. introvert
24. I have the patience for step-by-step work.	analytic vs. intuitive
25. I often seek out the company of others.	extrovert vs. introvert
26. I often act on my instincts.	analytic vs. intuitive
27. I adapt readily to the styles of those around me.	extrovert vs. introvert
28. I am usually well prepared.	analytic vs. intuitive
29. I am at my best when I can be spontaneous.	analytic vs. intuitive
30. I am comfortable sitting quietly and observing.	extrovert vs. introvert

Appendix B

Suggested Resources

About Personality and Temperament Styles

Many people have come up with ways to sort people into various personality types and styles. Each has its own particular slant. If this kind of thinking interests you, you might wish to explore these systems:

Strengths Finder 2.0 by Tom Rath, www.strengthsfinder.com

Keirsey Temperament Sorter, www.Keirsey.com

The DISC Personality System, www.discprofile.com

Myers-Briggs Type Indicator, www.Myersbriggs.org

About Asking for Gifts

Asking by Jerold Panas
Emerson and Church, 2009
www.emersonandchurch.com

Asking About Asking by M. Kent Stroman
CharityChannel Press, 2011
www.charitychannel.com

The Ask by Laura Fredricks
Jossey-Bass, 2010
www.joseybass.com

Other Books by Andrea Kihlstedt

Capital Campaigns: Strategies that Work
Jones and Bartlett Publishers, 2010
www.jbpub.com

How to Raise $1 Million (or More!) in 10 Bite-Sized Steps
Emerson & Church, 2010
www.emersonandchurch.com

Index

If you enjoyed this book, you'll want to pick up the other books in the CharityChannel Press In the Trenches™ series, shown on the following pages.

Also, we're introducing *Fundraising for the GENIUS,* which kicks off our new GENIUS series published by our imprint For the GENIUS Press. Visit http://ForTheGENIUS.com to learn more.

FUNDRAI$ING
as a Career:

What, Are You Crazy?

Linda Lysakowski, ACFRE

Practical answers for those:
- looking for a career change
- planning to hire development staff
- striving to advance in a development position

www.charitychannel.com

CharityChannel
PRESS

Trenches™

50 A$KS
in 50 Weeks

A Guide to Better Fundraising for Your Small Development Shop

Amy M. Eisenstein, CFRE

A Fundraising Planning Guide for:
- Development Professionals
- Nonprofit Executive Directors and CEOs
- Anyone else who wants to boost fundraising results

www.charitychannel.com

*Charity*Channel
PRESS™

IN THE

Trenches™

YOU AND YOUR
Nonprofit

Practical Advice and Tips from the

CharityChannel Professional Community

This is surely the book I wish I had decades ago.
—Bob Carter, Chair-elect, Association of
Fundraising Professionals (AFP)

Edited by:

Norman Olshansky
Linda Lysakowski, ACFRE

www.charitychannel.com

*Charity*Channel
PRESS™

IN THE

Trenches™

Capital Campaigns

Everything You NEED to Know

Linda Lysakowski, ACFRE

Discover how to:

- Conduct your capital campaign from start to finish
- Build a strong infrastructure for your campaign
- Develop a compelling campaign case statement
- Recruit volunteers for your campaign

www.charitychannel.com

*Charity*Channel
PRESS

Confessions of a Successful Grants Writer

A Complete Guide to Discovering and Obtaining Funding

Joanne Oppelt, MHA, GPC

A Guide for:

- Grant Writers
- Development Professionals
- Foundation, Corporate and Government Relationship Professionals
- Anyone Wanting to Raise More Revenue through Proposals

www.charitychannel.com

Charity Channel
PRESS

IN THE Trenches™

Getting Started in
Prospect Research

What you need to know
to find who you need to find

Meredith Hancks, MBA

For those who want to:

- Jump-start as a prospect researcher
- Create an optimal research tool kit
- Build vital relationships
- Use data to guide fundraising strategy

www.charitychannel.com

*Charity*Channel
PRESS

IN THE Trenches™

Raise More Money from Your Business Community

A Practical Guide to Tapping into Corporate Charitable Giving

Linda Lysakowski, ACFRE

Raise more money for your nonprofit organization by:

- Identifying the types of businesses likely to give
- Communicating with business leaders in a more compelling manner
- Involving volunteers from the business world in your fundraising activities

www.charitychannel.com

CharityChannel

PRESS™

IN THE

Trenches™

Raising More
with Less

An Essential Fundraising Guide for
Nonprofit Professionals and Board Members

Amy Eisenstein, CFRE

This book is ideal for:

- New fundraising professionals
- Professionals in small development shops
- Executive directors and board members who want to boost
  fundraising results

www.charitychannel.com

*Charity*Channel
PRESS™

And Introducing...

Fundraising

for the GENIUS ™

The only book you'll ever need
to raise more money for your
nonprofit organization.

FOR THE GENIUS IN ALL OF US ™

Linda Lysakowski, ACFRE

www.ForTheGENIUS.com

for the GENIUS ™
P R E S S

Made in the USA
San Bernardino, CA
04 August 2015